CW01311044

Indian Spring

**BY
BASANT NAIR**

Bloomington, IN   authorHOUSE   Milton Keynes, UK

AuthorHouse™
1663 Liberty Drive, Suite 200
Bloomington, IN 47403
www.authorhouse.com
Phone: 1-800-839-8640

AuthorHouse™ UK Ltd.
500 Avebury Boulevard
Central Milton Keynes, MK9 2BE
www.authorhouse.co.uk
Phone: 08001974150

© 2006 Basant Nair. All rights reserved.

No part of this book may be reproduced, stored in a retrieval system, or transmitted by any means without the written permission of the author.

First published by AuthorHouse 3/22/2006

ISBN: 1-4259-0946-9 (sc)

Printed in the United States of America
Bloomington, Indiana

This book is printed on acid-free paper.

*In memory of my parents
and my husband*

*I dedicate this book to
my children and their families*

Table of Contents

List of Illustrations	xi
Foreword	xiii
Acknowledgements	xvii
Preface	xxvii
My Parents and their Families	1
My Family and Early Childhood	9
Social and Cultural Activities	15
My Mother	23
Our Friends	31
My Growing Up Years and the National Movement	35
My College and University Days	43
On Holidays and Travels	49
My Brothers and Sisters	57
My Marriage	63
The War Years	77
My Most Difficult Days	83
I Resume a Normal Life Once Again	93

Independence and Partition	97
Some Unexpected Visitors	103
Partition and how it Affected our Families	107
Family Life after Partition	111
Delhi and Wellington	121
Back to Delhi and We Build a House	129
Kanpur Again	149
Another Difficult Chapter of My Life	153
The Nehru-Shastri Era 1947-1966	161
Praveen's Marriage	167
We Shift to Chandigarh	173
Pavan's Marriage	179
We Sell Our House	191
Trip to Vaishno Devi	199
Tega's Death and my Trip to Pune	203
Till Death Do Us Part	207
Malavika is Born and Pavan returns from Antarctica	219
Political Life 1967-1984	225
Indu's Marriage and My Trip to Khartoum	233

An Interlude in England	247
Praveen and R.K. Return from Lagos	253
Taiji Passes Away	255
N.P.'s Two Sisters	259
The Wedding Season	265
Visit to Solomon Islands	277
Life in Pune	285
Trip to Barbados	293
Tragedy Strikes	299
Radhika's Marriage	307
Departures	313
The Nehru Dynasty	317
Observations	329
Raheja Gardens	333
Reflections	335
Endnotes	343

List of Illustrations

India before Independence	xxiii
India after Independence	xxv
The Author's Father, Nand Lal Puri, 1942	5
The Author's Mother, Ishra Devi, 1942	6
The Author, Basant Nair, Pune, 2004	7
Narinjan Prasad Nair and Basant after their wedding, Calcutta 1941	71
Air Commodore N.P. Nair, 1964	72
Narinjan and Basant, Patiala Club, 1970	73
Family Photo on the occasion of Arvind's wedding, 1980	196
Nirmala and Basant at the Chattarpur Farm on Basant's Birthday, 2000	197
Major Pavan Nair receiving the Vishisht Seva Medal from Army Chief General Arun Vaidya, 1986	235
Malavika, Shyama, Pavan, Basant and Radhika in Pune, 1996	236
George, Indu and Marcus with Basant in Pune, 1996	237
Savita's Engagement, Delhi, 1992	270

The Marriage of Savita and Janardhan, Delhi, 1992	271
Praveen and Rajinder, 2004	272
Marcus and Prashant, 1994	273
Aryaman, 2003	274
Mateen and Radhika, 2001	311
Eesa and Umar, Oregon, 2005	312

Foreword

Basant was born in Lahore in 1919, as the sixth child of seven, at the time of the year when "the fields of mustard are in full bloom and the marigolds are in season". Her name signifies the advent of spring. Soon she moved to Calcutta when her father was appointed Manager of the Central Bank of India. After attending the Diocesan School run by Christian Missionaries, she joined the Ashutosh College for her BA degree, before entering Calcutta University, and became one of the few Indian women to earn a MA degree in Economics in that era. The insights of a Hindu woman, growing up in a closely-knit and traditional Punjabi family living in Bengal, are of considerable historical interest.

In her book, Basant, who is now 86, recounts the story of her family life against the background of events leading up to India's Independence. She recalls the trauma of the Jallianwala Bagh, the campaigns of Mahatma Gandhi, the advent of the Simon Commission, and the contribution of the Congress after the First

World War. The impact of Partition on her family and on India at large is graphically portrayed.

She remembers epic journeys to Burma, Singapore, China, and Japan in 1936, and to Kashmir and the famous Hindu shrine of Amarnath, high in the Himalayas, in 1940.

In 1941 she married Narinjan Prasad Nair, a dashing aeronautical engineer with the Madras Flying Club, who later went on to join the Air Force during the war, and subsequently became Air Commodore.

With her husband in the Air Force, Basant moved around India from Risalpur in North West Frontier Province to Kanpur in Uttar Pradesh, back to Risalpur, to Bhopal in Madhya Pradesh, Kolar in Karnataka, Ambala, to Kanpur (again), Delhi, Wellington, Delhi (again), and Kanpur (again). In all of these postings, Basant presents a vivid account of the lives of Air Force officers and their families, the clubs and the parties. Subsequently, when her husband N.P. was working for the Punjab and Haryana Governments, they lived in Patiala and then in Chandigarh.

Basant is able to share some of her most difficult moments of great personal tragedy, including the loss of her first child while her husband was in England, and the premature death of her daughter-in-law. She reflects on her husband's resignation from the Air Force and the sale of their Delhi house. As time progresses, new family members arrive, while others pass on. Her grand-daughter's conversion to Islam reveals an innermost struggle between religious conviction and family love. Now only Basant and her younger sister of the seven siblings survive, but she is consoled by her new role as grandmother, and great-grandmother.

While many of her age might be thinking of staying put in India, Basant continues her travels in her seventies, visiting Europe, Africa, the Pacific, and the Caribbean. Her trenchant observations of life in these countries are fascinating and always to the point.

Basant's history of her family from the beginnings of the 20th century to the present constitutes a unique portrayal of life in India viewed from the perspective of a daughter, wife, mother, and grandmother. Her commentary on the Nehru dynasty is profound in its analysis and gives a good insight into a thinking citizen's appreciation of Indian politics.

This is a book for those interested in India's remarkable progression during the last century.

George Gwyer
Hove, April 2005

Acknowledgements

I have to thank Rajinder, my elder son-in-law, for suggesting that I should start writing at leisure. I liked the idea and decided on writing my memoirs.

If this book is printed or published, some part of the credit goes to my younger son-in-law George. He not only encouraged me to write but also put my writing on the computer, not once but several times when I chose to add a paragraph or delete a sentence. He may have corrected a spelling or grammatical mistake but otherwise did not change a single word of what I wrote. I marvelled at his patience. My children Praveen, Pavan and Indu, read parts of the draft occasionally and gave some suggestions which I have tried to incorporate. Indu helped in editing the script and Pavan went though the whole manuscript on more than one occasion. I owe them all a big thank you for bringing it to this final stage. If there are any omissions concerning family members and events, or other people whom I have been privileged to know,

I ask for their understanding. I have expressed my personal opinions but readers are at liberty to differ.

It is customary in India to pay obeisance to one's Guru before presenting anything to the public. Thus I take this opportunity of paying homage to my two English teachers who taught me to read, write and speak English. They were two British women, Miss Bell Chambers and Ms Gwen MacMillan, my teachers at the Missionary School in Calcutta. I always had great regard for Sister Dorothy Francis C.S.J.B. who was the Principal of the School.

My thanks go also to the publishers.

My Father's Family Tree

Lala Ralia Ram Puri (grandfather)
m. Radha (grandmother)

Madhu Sudan Lal ----- Nand Lal Puri ----- Manohar Lal --- Saraswati Devi
                      m. Ishra Devi (mother)

Som Prakash	Sukh Dev	Sarup	Shakti	Sarla	Basant	Nirmala
m. Kunti	m. Kamla	m. Lalo	m. Savitri	m. KC Khosla	m. NP Nair	m. HK Kapur
Arjun	Tripta, Krishna Nita, Rupa	Saroj, Raghu	Surrinder, Narinder, Asha, Vijay	Kusum, Tara Rajen, Sumen		Madhu Arvind, Som

My Husband's Family Tree

Dewan Dilbagh Rai (grandfather)
m. (name unknown)

Mahesh Das -----	Durga Prasad Nair----- Pratap Kaur (mother)	Sohanlal ---	Kedar Nath ----	Shambu Nath
Kaushalya Devi ------ m. Durga Prasad Sodh	Prakash Vati ----- m. Prakash Chand Varma	Ram Prasad ------- m. Chand	Krishan Prasad----- m. Rajan	Narinjan Prasad m. Basant
Kanta, Suraj, Jagdish Santosh, Brijmohan Bimla, Inder, Ashok Vinod, Kiran, Ajit	Chander, Inder, Sheila		Uma, Vijai, Vinod Viveik, Litllue	Praveen, Pavan, Indu

My Family Tree

Narinjan Prasad Nair (husband)
m. Basant Puri

- Praveen -----
  m. Rajinder Kumar Khanna
- Savita -----
  m. Janardhan Kapur
  - Aryaman
- Prashant
- Pavan -----
  m. Shyama Kher
  - Radhika -----
    m. Mateen Khan
    - Eesa   Umar
  - Malavika
- Indu -----
  m. George Gwyer
  - Marcus

Footnote: My husband's surname Nair gives an impression that he was a South Indian, but actually he was a Punjabi Khatri. The name should have been spelt Nayyar, but my father-in-law spelt the name in English as Nair. When his children grew up their names were registered in school as sons of D.P. Nair. Thus the spelling has stuck to this day. So there is now a very small group of Punjabi Nairs.

INDIA BEFORE INDEPENDENCE

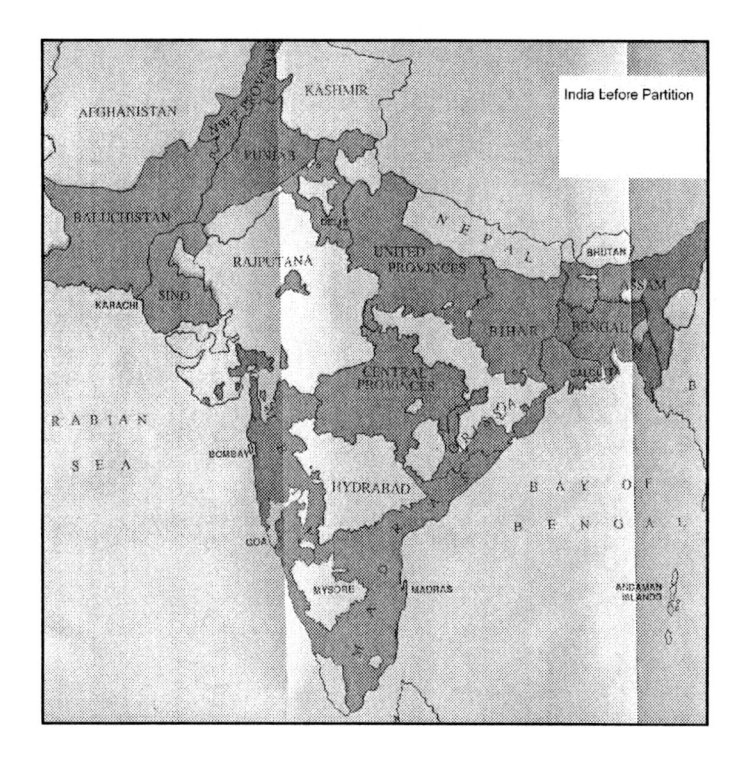

Source: Columbia University, New York

INDIA AFTER INDEPENDENCE

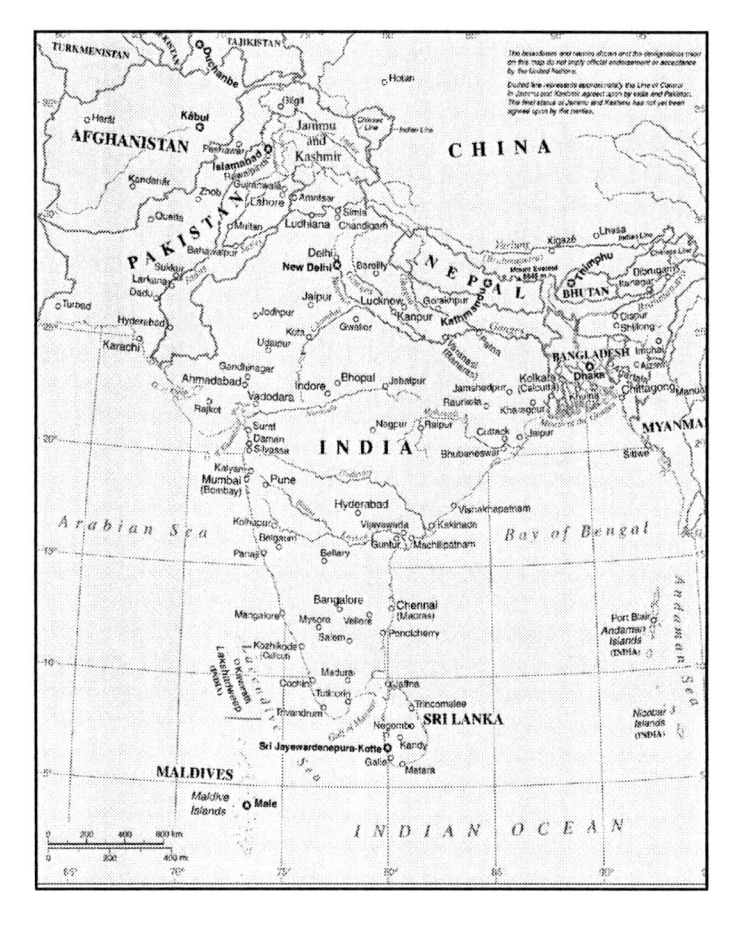

Source: United Nations, Department of Peacekeeping Operations, Cartographic Section, Map No. 4140 Rev 3, January 2004.

Preface

I am eighty-six years old. Slowly and steadily my body is giving way. I have a tendency towards high blood pressure, both my eyes have been successfully operated for cataracts. When I say, *"I am a little short of hearing"*, my children laughingly retort, *"But Mummy, you are quite deaf, you should wear your hearing aid"*. I now have a little heart problem also, mild diabetes, and arthritis which has attacked my knees. I am really not perturbed for I know it is just a price one has to pay for living so long. I have generally enjoyed good health and am happy that the doctors so far have not made any adverse comments on my mental faculties.

After living with my son Pavan and his family for nineteen years, I am now living by myself in a flat in Raheja Gardens, Pune, which belongs to my daughter and son-in-law, Indu and George, who have their permanent home in England. I find the flat very comfortable and convenient, it is very central, it has a lift and is close to Salunke Vihar where Pavan lives, and so I also have his support.

I have plenty of free time and find myself thinking about the past. So while I am still of sound mind and have a good memory, I thought I would write a sort of autobiography or memoirs, which may not be of much value to the public, but my children, grand- children, and great grand-children, may find it interesting to get a picture, not only of my life and a little knowledge about their ancestors, but also to get an idea of the social and political atmosphere of India after the 1st World War. I have no intention of going into any research; whatever I am recording is from my memory. The events that had a profound effect on the people of India are clearly etched on my mind. Since I am not writing the history of Indian independence and am only touching on the political side, many luminaries have not been mentioned. This in no way means any disrespect to them.

The best time to write one's autobiography or memoirs is when one stops looking forward to life and spends more time rambling down memory lane, and more or less, relives the pleasure and pains of the past.

I have skipped some unpleasant incidents, because they may reflect badly on some living and some dead. I have no intention of hurting anyone's feelings. If I have felt hurt, the pain ultimately has helped me to become more contemplative and philosophical, and I find myself at peace.

I am in the last stage of my life and moving towards a new dawn that God has ordained for me; because I do believe in the transmigration of the soul. For now my prayer is for God to give me a peaceful end, so that I am no burden to my children.

My Parents and their Families

I was born in Lahore (now in Pakistan) on Basant Panchmi, 5 February 1919. It is a festival of celebrating the season of Spring. At this time of the year, the fields of mustard are in full bloom and look beautiful with bright yellow flowers. The marigolds are in season and the fragrant Champa and Chameli[1] have their own charm. On this day women wear yellow clothes and men yellow turbans. Young boys come out in the sunshine and kite-flying is the sport of the day. Yellow sweet rice is cooked with saffron and dry fruits, and there is a sense of happiness all around. Over the years, men have stopped wearing yellow turbans and kite-flying is now not so popular, for it has been replaced by several other games. In spite of these changes, the day is always considered very auspicious and the general mood is of happiness. In Bengal, the same day is celebrated as Saraswati Puja, worshipping the Goddess of learning. One can see the enthusiasm of the student community busy with their preparations for pending examinations which are generally held in March. The girls also wear yellow on that day. My parents did not have to look for a name for me: they just called me Basant. The day of the festival changes each year, but I have always celebrated my birthday on the day of the festival.

My Father, Lala Nandlal Puri[2] hailed from a small village Ghartal near Sialkot in Punjab. He was amongst the early Punjabis to become a Bachelor of Law. He tried to set up a legal practice but was not successful. So he took up employment with the Punjab National Bank, the first Indian private bank of Punjab, and was posted in Lahore. He had an elder brother who was not highly educated and a sister who was illiterate. His younger brother was also a graduate and joined as a police officer in the service of the Nizam of Hyderabad.

My Mother Ishra Devi Sobti was the third daughter of Lala Lachman Das who belonged to Gujrat, a town 40 to 50 miles from Lahore. The eldest daughter was married to one of the Dewans of Kashmir and the second married into a well-to-do landlord family of Sialkot. Neither of the two sons in-law was educated in the formal sense – they may have gone to school or studied privately – but they were very prosperous. Both the sisters adjusted into being obedient daughters-in-law, observing purdah, having children and acting in a traditional way of being door mats to their families. My grandfather was now keen to have an educated groom for the third daughter. My Chachi[3] was distantly related to my Mother, spoke very highly of my Father who had just lost his first wife. *"Your daughter will be very happy, he is a fine man."*

Thus my Father, a thirty two years old, plain looking man, deeply influenced by Arya Samaj[4], with a seven years old daughter, got married to my Mother, a lovely robust girl of sixteen, who could just about read, and write a little *gurumukhe*[5].

My Mother had a younger sister who was engaged to a medical student, Jagat Ram Kochar, whose family was also in Gujrat. My grandfather unfortunately died before she was married, and my grandmother had died even before my Mother's marriage. So my aunt spent a few months with my Mother till she got married. Father had an independent establishment in Lahore (my grandparents were in Sargodha). The elder sisters were in joint families and it was not customary to have a wife's relatives living in. Even after her marriage, when uncle had qualified as a doctor and joined the Army and was posted in Mesopotamia during the first World War, my aunt, with her two children, divided her time between my Mother and her own in-laws. This was my Mother's first blessing that she was able to have her younger sister with her, without any inhibitions. We were always very close to the Kochar family.

I never saw my half-sister who was married while still in her teens and died giving birth to a still-born child, leaving behind a two years old son. Her husband remarried a cousin of his late wife from her Mother's side. So the burden of bringing up that child did not fall on my parents. Very cordial relations existed between the two families. When this nephew grew up, Father helped to find him a good job and we attended his wedding with generous gifts as befitted Father's position. He later also joined my brother's business.

THE AUTHOR'S FATHER,
NAND LAL PURI, 1942

THE AUTHOR'S MOTHER,
ISHRA DEVI, 1942

THE AUTHOR,
BASANT NAIR, PUNE, 2004

My Family and Early Childhood

I was the sixth child of my parents. Mother gave birth to four sons and a daughter within seven years of her marriage, and I was born after a gap of five years. Another sister Nirmala arrived when I was four years old.

I was a year old when Father left the Punjab National Bank and joined the Central Bank. It was a Parsi bank with its headquarters in Bombay (Mumbai). They wanted to open a branch in Lahore. The Managing Director approached Father to join them and promised him a big rise in his salary. Father thought it over and told the Punjab National Bank that he had this offer; if they gave him a little rise he would not consider the new offer. The Bank refused, and Father resigned out of sheer self-respect.

He opened the Central Bank branch in Lahore and was able to show a small profit in the first year. The Bank now wanted him to go to Calcutta (Kolkata) and manage the branches there. They offered him very attractive terms, but Father was very reluctant to leave Lahore. He had never travelled anywhere except in the Punjab. Bengal was like a distant foreign country, with an altogether different language and culture. He had four school-going sons and he did not want to take any risk. The Managing Director then suggested that he should leave his family in Lahore and go to Calcutta alone for six months, and if he liked it he could stay on, otherwise he could return to the Lahore branch. Father could not refuse, he went to Calcutta and after three months asked the Bank if his wife and children could join him for a month as the children had holidays. The Bank very readily agreed to pay the railway fares for the family. It was a journey of forty hours, with a change at Mogulsarai. There was no question of Mother travelling alone with six children, so a brother of my aunt accompanied her, to make the journey safe and comfortable. Mother liked Calcutta very much and the terms offered by the Bank were so attractive that Father decided to stay on. For the next 27 years he worked for the Bank, and retired at the age of seventy-two. He continued to live in Calcutta till he passed away at the age of eighty in 1955.

My eldest brother, Som Prakash[6], was about thirteen years old. He was left in Lahore with a cousin of Father's to do his schooling in Lahore, and five of us were in Calcutta. I was then 3 years old. My earliest memory is of our house that Father rented, 37 Hazra Road in South Calcutta, while his office was in Clive Street, the hub of commercial life in North Calcutta. Father bought a car and engaged a chauffeur: he was not inclined to learn driving. My three brothers went to an Indian school, which was right opposite the first house he had rented on his arrival in Calcutta. It was a Bengali School, but English was taught and there was provision for Urdu also. So my three brothers matriculated from there: the two elder boys went on to St. Xavier's in Calcutta, and the Shaktiji[7] went to Government College Lahore.

Father was not in favour of the convent schools for girls where English was taught and stress was laid on French and Latin. It was the fashion for all the well-to-do people to send their daughters to the convents. There were hardly any Indian schools available for girls. Someone recommended the Diocesan Collegiate School, which was also a Christian Missionary School. The medium of teaching was Bengali for junior classes, but English was taught from the beginning, and Sanskrit was taught as a classical language. The Principal had a reputation for not forcing Chapel and Bible studies, which were optional. The girls came from middle class Bengali families. Sarlabibi, my elder sister, went to this school. The Principal was very happy to have a non-Bengali girl and told Father that she would be very happy to introduce Hindi teaching if there were a few more non-Bengali girls joining the school. Within a short period, many girls who wanted to do Hindi also joined the school and a Hindi teacher was employed.

The Gokhale Memorial School was established and Father was their banker. Mrs P.C. Ray, wife of a very highly respected professor, worked tirelessly for the school and insisted *"Mr. Puri, your daughter must come to our school"*, and Sarlabibi, who was then in the 7th class, shifted to this school. I was picking up Bengali fast, and was quite happy and did not want a change. My younger sister Nirmala later went to the Gokhale also with Sarlabibi, who was older and considered more responsible.

Nirmala was about seven years old and I was eleven. We were both playing in the courtyard when we saw two kites flying and we became interested and excited about them. The kites suddenly disappeared, and I thought that if we went up to the roof, we would be able to see better. So we both ran up (we were actually forbidden to go to the roof as it did not have a parapet and was unsafe). We were both quite excited,

Nirmala got to the edge and was going round in circles and clapping her hands. Before I was able to get her away from the edge, she fell and I shouted and ran. Mother saw her falling and rushed downstairs to find her in the arms of a stranger, who saw her falling from the road, and rushed to the front courtyard and caught her in his arms. He just put her in Mother's arms and disappeared. Nirmala seemed perfectly alright except for a little bruise on her arm which had brushed against a tree. Her first words to Mother were *"Don't worry Mother, God has saved me with His Own Hands"*. I must mention here that the line she used was out of a song that Mother used to sing, the purport of which was that God's hands can work wonders. She was taken to the hospital for a thorough check up. She was just fine. The incident left a deep impression on me. I really felt that God had come to help me. I would never have forgiven myself if something had happened to her. After that day I never disobeyed my parents.

Social and Cultural Activities

When Father went to Calcutta, the European community was controlling the jute, tea and the coal business. They only dealt with the Imperial Bank, which was a Government bank. There were, however, big Marwari and Parsi communities, and of course a few big Bengali business houses, which dealt with the Central Bank. By the time Father was well established, there were several Punjabis holding top government jobs and a few doing well in business also. The Oberois (of hotel fame), Malhotras (Topaz) and the Thapars, became big industrialists. In short, there was a fairly big Punjabi community who formed an important section of the society of Calcutta.

Father now wanted to do some social work. A new Arya Samaj was set up in Bhawanipore, South Calcutta. There was a Samaj in Bura Bazaar, but people found it difficult to go so far. Pandit Rishi Ram, a very learned man, took charge and every Wednesday there was a *Havan*[8], *Bhajans*[9], and then a discourse. There was a big response and soon Sunday classes for children were also organized. Every Friday there would be a gathering in any member's house who desired to have a Havan. In short, the people of South Calcutta found a priest for their weddings and other ceremonies (including funerals) without any difficulty.

The influence of Arya Samaj was felt in the Punjab, Gujarat and Uttar Pradesh. The Bramoho Samaj, which was started by Raja Ram Mohan Roy, had a profound effect in Bengal. Both were reformist movements based on religion. The main difference was that Swami Dayanand laid stress on the Vedas and advocated Hindi as the national language and learning Sanskrit, the Bramohos were more influenced by western philosophy.

The Rama Krishna Mission was typically Hindu, as their preceptor was Shri Rama Krishna who was illiterate and a devotee of Kali. He was able to influence the most intelligent people of his time with his wise observations. Swami Vivekananada, who started the Rama Krishna Mission for serving the people, is well known. The Mission has given yeomanly service to the nation in the fields of education, health, famine relief, and other social activities.

Father was responsible for opening a Kanya Vidyalaya[10], where the medium of instruction was Hindi with very nominal fees. On the sports side, he was able to get permission for a tennis Club in the Woodburn Park, where the South Club already existed (where all the international tournaments are held even now). So the Punjab Club was started to enable the Punjabi families to learn and play tennis. A whole group of people from Madras were also keen to have a similar club, but could not muster up enough members. They approached Father who very willingly accepted them as members. As time passed the Punjabis wanted to add some social activities and a small flat was rented for people to get together in the evenings for indoor games and bridge. Then came a time that the members wanted to have alcohol served in the club for which a license was required. In the general meeting the group that wanted alcohol won, and Father resigned. The club wanted to have a picture of Father, as a respect to the founder member, but he refused; he did not want his picture in a club where alcohol was served. Today it is one of the very well known clubs of Calcutta. Much later, my third brother Sarupji became the President also.

As far as our education was concerned, besides going to school, we were encouraged to play badminton every evening in our compound. My brothers went for swimming. Whenever we went to the hills, usually Darjeeling, we did a lot of riding and roller-skating. Long walks and picnics formed an important part of our programmes. What was really most enjoyable was the fact that we were always three or four families who would rent a few bungalows, and spend a lot of time together.

Father was in favour of educating his daughters but I do not think it occurred to him that we should be career oriented and be able to earn a living and be financially independent. He was traditional enough to spend more on the education of his sons to enable them to get good jobs. He was equally keen to find good homes for his daughters and give them away in marriage to qualified young men. There were not many openings, even for the men. The Indian Civil Service and the Army were considered prestigious followed by medicine, law, engineering and education. Thus when my two brothers went to England for banking it was considered quite unusual. Slowly new avenues were opening like civil aviation and the film industry.

Most of Father's friends, especially the men in Government service, were more Anglophone. When one of them sent his daughters to the Calcutta School of Music for violin and piano classes, Father engaged a Bengali musician, who came to the house twice a week to teach Indian classical music to my sister Sarla. She had a soft melodious voice and picked up singing in no time. She excelled in Indian singing. I sometimes wonder, if a girl had that sort of voice and ear for music now, she would be recognized as a genius, and every effort would be made by the parents to go in for intensive learning from the best music teachers. But things were different then and she specialized in *Bhajans* and rendered them with great feeling. She also went to painting classes that a French lady used to conduct.

All this was happening when she was about fourteen and fifteen and I was ten. I heard a lot of music and saw a lot of painting, which helped me to develop a good ear for music. I had a very good memory and would know the words of all the songs by heart. What I did not develop was my voice. Similarly I got to know a lot about paints, how they were to be used and mixed, what brushes were for different effects, but never got down to painting. However, my only strong point was my studies. I knew and remembered everything I was taught. I paid full attention in class and did not have to learn my lessons. My parents were very happy with my school reports, and did not insist on my spending time on painting and music. I now sometimes wish that had they insisted, I may not have been as good as

Sarlabibi, but I could have learnt more. It was clear that she was inclined towards the arts while I was more towards studies and books. The latest trend then was to allow children to develop their own interests.

Mention must be made of two young Punjabis: Kundan Lal Saigal and Prithvi Raj Kapoor who came to Calcutta with letters of introduction from Father's friends. They wanted to join the film industry. Saigal was a singer with no formal training, and Prithvi Raj was interested in acting. Father sent them both to B.N. Sarkar, proprietor of New Theatres, requesting him to give these young men an opportunity. They did not come together, but more or less at the same time. They both achieved significant success. It was more difficult for Saigal because he had to act also. There was no playback singing then. They both created a sensation and became celebrities overnight. Saigal's song of Chandidas and Devdas still ring in people's ears. In a short span of less than 10 years he had made himself immortal. He died in 1947 after he had moved to Bombay. Lata Mangeskar has had a span of more than half a century and she deserves all the fame and popularity, but Saigal in much less time will go down in the history of film music and should be placed at par with her. Prithvi Raj, besides being a good actor, was a great thinker also and did some memorable roles, and later became a member of the Rajya Sabha. His sons Raj Kapoor, Shammi, and Shashi followed in his footsteps and now Prithvi Raj's grandsons and great-grand daughters are very much in the limelight of the film world. One cannot think of Bollywood without the Kapoor family.

My Mother

Quite late in my life I realized that my Mother hardly ever referred to her parents. I was able to discern that she came from a well-to-do family, because both the elder sisters were married into rich families. She did not have a brother, and all the property of my grandfather must have gone to his brothers and nephews. The law was that the daughters could not inherit the property, they were entitled to only *Stree Dhan*[11].

She had great regard for her husband and could foresee what was required of her and would always rise to an occasion. Father was kind and considerate to her and appreciated her qualities of truthfulness and strong common sense. He always consulted her on any big decisions that had to be made. His vital decisions of joining the Central Bank and then shifting to Calcutta were very much influenced by her.

She was generous and wise. This can be measured

by the following incident. Father had rented a double storied house consisting of ten rooms, two large verandahs, and a courtyard in front, as well as one at the back. There was a long wall separating the house with a door to enter into another courtyard which had one room (meant for fodder) and a shed for cows. The house had belonged to a big zamindar[12] who had several sons. This property came to a son who was now holding a clerical job, and had three daughters and a son. He was finding it difficult to make two ends meet. He came to the house one day and requested Father to increase the rent, as he himself was living in a rented house and found it difficult to maintain the family. Mother very spontaneously suggested that *"Instead of raising the rent, why don't you build a few rooms in the back courtyard and save the rent that you pay, besides you will have the pleasure of living in your own house"*. The answer was *"Where will I get the money for building the rooms?"* to which Mother said *"We will give you an advance, and you can pay it back slowly"*.

Father was a bit surprised but did not say anything. When the gentleman left he said, *"What made you take such a bold step? He may ask for a big sum and I may not be able to give it"*.

Her answer was *"I am not asking your bank to give the loan. You will give the amount. He is a very decent man, he will pay back every penny and if he can't we shall raise the rent also. They should really be living in this house. It is his father's property."*

Mother ran a very good home, where simple wholesome Punjabi food was served. As Mother did not speak or understand Bengali, even the servants were either from Punjab or Uttar Pradesh. A Bengali Ayah[13] was employed when my younger sister was born, as she found it a big responsibility to get a woman servant from Punjab. Punjabi was spoken in the house. She welcomed guests, feeding one or two extra people without any notice never posed a problem. There was a big tandoor[14] in the house. Many a friend would take it for granted that they would eat with us, with or without any notice, whenever they came. Since she was invited to parties where European food was served, she would not hesitate to ask how a dish was made if she liked it. Thus fried Bekti[15] and chips, and simple sweet dishes like baked caramel custard, fruit salads, jellies and ice creams were introduced besides the Indian puddings of halwas and kheers. She did not have the occasion of eating much Bengali food, but Bengali sweets were very popular because there were plenty of shops where the famous Rasgollas and Sandesh were easily available.

Mother was extremely fond of good clothes and jewellery. She had a great flair for designing jewellery, and would suggest changes which even the jewellers appreciated. She never hesitated to buy sarees if she liked them, and always had a box full of new sarees which would readily come out and be given away as presents. She never had a bank account or a joint account; the bills just went to Father and he paid them. She always knew how much to spend and never gave Father an opportunity to complain.

Occasionally she went to Punjab to meet her relatives and on one such occasion she met her niece (her sister's daughter) in Sialkot. Her sister had died and the brother-in-law had remarried. This niece was about sixteen years old; she was not going to school and spoke little English. Mother told her brother-in-law that she would like to take her niece to Calcutta for sometime. He readily agreed. So Pushpabibi, as we called her, came and stayed with us for nearly two years. She was six months younger than my elder sister. She was too old to join a school but a special European teacher was engaged to teach her English. Pushpabibi benefited a lot, she was extremely pretty, and very soon she got into wearing sarees. For her it was like going to a finishing school, learning English, having music lessons, playing badminton. After a couple of years she was married to Maluk Singh Bedi, a tall handsome Sikh whose father, Baba Ladha Singh, was a very successful contractor in Calcutta, and had coal collieries in Asansol. She was treated like a daughter with a lot of love and affection, and she always reciprocated.

Although Father was an Arya Samaji, my Mother had a copy of 'Durbar Sahib' the Sikh sacred book, because she knew the Punjabi script, and Father never objected. She had respect for all religions, she would always say *"If India can boast of Hindu religion and say Rama and Krishna were incarnations of God, then God who created the whole universe may have sent the prophets to other parts of the world also. All the Christians and Muslims are no fools who believe in Christ and Muhammad"*. Were the seeds of respecting all religions sown by her, for we now have a Christian and a Muslim in the family who are very dear to us.

We were celebrating the festival of Holi in 1937. We had a most enjoyable morning, playing with colours, eating, drinking, singing and dancing. We were all quite tired and wanted a good rest after lunch. Suddenly we found Mother feeling very uncomfortable and saying *"I am feeling as if half my body is burning"*. We all tried to laugh it off, but soon realized that she was indeed in great agony. I tried to give her a cold sponge and apply talcum powder. Father wanted to call in a doctor. He thought it must be some allergy that she had got with the colours that were used in the morning. But she insisted that *"Only half my body is burning"*. She had tears rolling down her cheeks. We stood together quite helpless for nothing seemed to work. As the evening approached she fell off in a doze. A telegram arrived saying Masiji, Mother's younger sister Mrs Kochar, had died and the funeral had already taken place. The time coincided when her sister was on the funeral pyre. She was going through the agony of feeling the burning sensation. Is there any explanation for this?

When my aunt died only two of her children were settled. Raj Kumari was married to Captain Srinagesh who eventually rose to be the Chief of the Army staff. Raj Kumar had just returned from Sandhurst and was a King's commissioned officer in the Indian Army. Both these children were born before the First World War. At that time the other eight children ranged in age from two to seventeen. Over the next five years my Mother (she died in 1943) was able to arrange the marriages of two of her nieces. Bubbley got married to Jagdish Chopra who had just returned after graduating from Cambridge and was the younger brother of my sister-in-law Kuntibibi. He held an excellent job with Burmah Shell. I cannot resist saying that Bubbley was one of the most beautiful girls that I have ever seen. After about sixty years I think that the only face that looks like hers is Aishwarya Rai who was declared Miss World and is now a very popular actress. Tiny got married to Kawal Raj Puri, a grandson of my father's cousin. He ultimately attained the post of the Governor of the Reserve Bank of India.

I always remember Maluk Singhji describing Mother, saying *"In her last life she must have been Akbar Badshah[16]. She is gracious, intelligent, tolerant, ever-helpful, with a keen sense of humour, ready to enjoy good things of life"*.

Our Friends

As Mother did not speak English or Bengali, many of the family friends were Punjabis. The atmosphere of the house was Anglophone only to the extent of having a proper drawing room, while the dining room was equipped with all the necessary crockery and cutlery. Basically it was a Punjabi household, but both Nirmala and I had a big dose of Bengali culture. The girls in our school were Bengalis: we were speaking fluent Bengali. Our real contact with Bengali culture came when the landlord's family shifted into the back courtyard. Their elder daughters were of our age and we were never discouraged from going into their house. Thus we became very good friends. The elder girl went to a local Bengali school, but we persuaded the younger girl to go to the same school as Nirmala and all the years we were there, she used to go and return from school with Nirmala in our car. Mrs. Roy, the Mother, was a very sweet lady and loved to have us with her and she always tried to give us some

Bengali preparations which she had made herself. I always remember receiving a lot of love and affection from her, and we used to call her "Ma" just as her own children. We developed a taste for Bengali food which was cooked in mustard oil. The meals were generally served in *Thalis*[17] and would consist of something fried like a piece of brinjal, then a dry curry, fish curry with boiled rice. Curd was hardly ever served, and if at all, it was as a sweet. We became very familiar with their customs as we used to attend our friends' birthdays and marriages. This friendship lasted for several years, till both our friends got married and we shifted to our own house in Mandeville Gardens in 1936.

I remember our parents' friends, the Bhandaris, the Chopras, Bedis, Lalchands, who all had children more or less our age and I remember that whenever we went for holidays to Darjeeling, we were generally together. Father and Mr Bhandari, Accountant General of Bengal, were close friends, but temperamentally poles apart. Mr. Bhandari wanted to go duck shooting, but Father would not agree.

Then he persuaded him to start playing golf, and Father tried his hand but found it very time consuming, so that also did not work. Then Mr. Bhandari wanted to teach him bridge. Since bridge was a card game and could be played at home, Mother also decided to learn. Both my parents never read any book on bridge, but learnt a few main conventions and started playing auction bridge. When I was about twelve years old, they had switched on to contract bridge with the Culbertson conventions, later on Blackwood and Crain also. I started bridge when I was fourteen.

After having had so many children in quick succession, my Mother had really lost her health. While she had aches and pains, she never lost her zeal for life. She enjoyed playing bridge and every evening, two or three friends were invited to the house. Even if she was not well enough to play, her bed was put in the verandah and there would be a foursome. Light refreshments were always provided. If a guest thanked her for her hospitality, she would always say *"You are doing me a favour by coming to our house, otherwise either he would be bored or I would be left on my own"*.

My Growing Up Years and the National Movement

I was familiar with the phrase *Jallianwala Bagh* right from the age of 3 or 4, as far as I can throw back my memory. Whenever anybody asked my age, Mother would always say Basant was about two and a half months old when the Jallianwala Bagh tragedy occurred.

On 13 April 1919, there was supposed to be a big *Jalsa* in Amritsar in the Jallianwala Bagh[18]. General Dyer wanted the function to be banned. It was Baisakhi Day[19] and thousands of men and women had gathered. General Dyer first got all the gates shut and then ordered indiscriminate firing. Hundreds died. In a stampede to escape, women and children were crushed to death. Hundreds were injured. Next day Martial Law was declared and soon after the Rowlatt Act was passed, which was extremely derogatory and insulting to Indians. Hundreds perished but the incident gave a strong impetus to the Independence movement. So far it was only the educated, intelligentsia with western education leading the Congress with petitions, prayers and protests. Now it became a national movement, as the common people realized the grave injustice of being ruled by foreigners. Mahatma Gandhi also came on the scene at this time.

I think I was about 10 years old when Sir Michael O'Dwyer was shot dead in England by a young Sikh, Udham Singh. I heard my Father say, *"Good, he deserved to be shot"*. I was surprised to hear my Father say *"Good'* when some one was killed. Thus I made up my mind to find out more about the incident.

My next memory is when Mahatma Gandhi gave a call of giving up the use of all foreign goods and get down to *Charkha*[20]. People started making bonfires of foreign clothes. Mother did not approve of this *tamasha*[21]. *"Is this not national wealth that is being burnt. Make up your mind not to buy foreign goods in future"*, she said.

In the Punjab which was a cotton growing region also, it was quite customary for girls and women folk to make thread on the spinning wheel and then weave *khes and durries*[22]. In winter the women would sit out in the sun to work together. There were a lot of the songs in which *Charkha* was the central theme. My Mother had a *Charkha* lying in the box room. It was taken out and we all thought that it was great fun trying to make thread. Mother was the only one who could really spin out thin thread and she would always sing when spinning. This movement led to the closing down of the Lancashire mills. Round table conferences were called, but always failed.

Then came the Simon Commission in 1931. Mahatmaji gave a call to boycott it. Lala Lajpat Rai was leading a procession as a protest in Lahore, there was a *lathi*[23] charge to disperse the crowd and Lalaji was specially selected to receive several blows on the head. He died in the hospital and his last words were *"every blow dealt to me is a nail in the coffin of the British Empire".*

As a sign of disobedience, Mahatma Gandhi chose to make salt from seawater (making salt from seawater was prohibited). There was a small salt tax levied by the Government which yielded a large amount. Gandhi said that it was an unfair tax because it taxed the extremely poor, children and old people, who consumed salt. It was against all canons of economics to tax people on the bare necessities of life. The movement captured the imagination of the people and thousands participated as Gandhi started his walk to Dandee in March 1930 to make salt. The Government could not possibly arrest all the people, so hundreds of them would be put in lorries, driven about 20 or 30 miles away, and left there to walk back. The procession continued to swell until they reached Dandee on 7 April 1930. It was the most successful non-violent effort of civil disobedience. Sixty thousand people were arrested and Mahatma Gandhi was put in jail.

At this time there was also a strong movement wanting to use force against the British, by a secret terrorist movement which was very strong in Bengal. Several bomb incidents occurred. Mahatma Gandhi never approved of this school of thought. The youth did not believe non-violence could be effective against the British. The people also thought that what they said made sense and were considered heroes and patriots. The story of Sardar Bhagat Singh, a youth of 23 years, is relevant. He threw a bomb in the legislative assembly, was caught red-handed and then he, with Sukhdev and Rajguru, was hanged. A student of my College (when I was still in school) went to receive her BA degree at the convocation where the Governor was to hand over the degrees. She attempted to shoot the Governor with a pistol at close range when she went up to receive her degree. This was Bina Das, a young girl of 20, who was sent for seven years rigorous imprisonment. The Governor escaped unhurt.

Bengal was the first State to be westernized and take up the western ways. It was also the earliest to get into the national movement. On the cultural side, there were the Brahmo Samaj and Shri Rama Krishna, whose disciple Swami Vivekananda made a great impact in India. Then there were people like Aurobindo Ghosh and Rabindranath Tagore who created history. W.C. Bonnerjee was the first Indian President of the Indian National Congress. Bipin Chander Pal of Bengal, Bal Gangadhar Tilak from Maharashtra, and Lala Lajpat Rai from Punjab led the national movement. It is interesting to note that the women of Bengal were the first to join the national movement also. I had the good fortune to see women like Sarojini Naidu, Kamala Devi Chattopadhaya, Aruna Asaf Ali and Sucheta Kriplani working with Mahatma Gandhi. The Nehru family came into prominence when Motilal Nehru took to politics in the early twenties.

C. R. Das of Bengal was an eminent lawyer and member of the Congress. His views were more radical than those of Mahatma Gandhi. He had great regard for the Mahatma but chose to form a Swarajist Party within the Congress with the support of Motilal Nehru. Subhash Bose, who was much younger, became the disciple of C.R. Das and in favour of active opposition to the British Raj, in contrast to Gandhi's principles of passive resistance and non-cooperation. After C.R. Das and Motilal Nehru passed away, Bose now represented their school of thought of direct action. I was a child when Das died but I always knew he was a great patriot who was called *Desh Bandhu* or friend of the nation. A charitable hospital was opened in his memory called the Chitaranjan Seva Sadan. Much later, the cancer ward was added for which my father played a major role in collecting funds.

In 1939 came the Second World War. The Congress was now a very powerful body, but the Muslim League under the leadership of Mohammad Ali Jinnah was also a formidable force and always took a stand against the Congress. Mahatmaji was in favour of non-violence, non-cooperation, and civil disobedience. Another school of thought was in favour of action. Subhash Chandra Bose belonged to this group and was elected the President (he was extremely popular with the masses) but was not able to form a working committee so he resigned. I attended this session of the Congress in Ramgarh and felt very sad for him. But he created history when he was put under house arrest. He was able to escape and travel incognito from Calcutta to Lahore, Peshawar and then through Afghanistan to Germany. There he met Hitler and proceeded to Singapore and formed the Indian National Army, with Indian army personnel who had been taken prisoners by the Japanese, to fight the British alongside the Japanese.

I got married in 1941 and I will develop the theme of Independence subsequently.

My College and University Days

By the time I had passed my tenth grade, and was ready to join a college, three of my brothers and Sarlabibi were married, and Arjun, Kusum and Tripta were born. This was a sort of new phase for me, having little nephews and nieces, loving them, cuddling them and enjoying playing with them. In 1936, Father bought a house in Mandeville Gardens, and life changed even more. The landlord's family was now left behind, the days of long drives and picnics became less frequent. Thus by the time I was in first year college, I developed the habit of reading. I was reading Jayne Eyre, Wuthering Heights, Little Women, a translation of Victor Hugo's *Les Miserables*, Tolstoy's Anna Karenina. I knew enough Bengali to read Bankim Chatterjee, Tagore, Sarat Chatterjee, and works of Munshi Premchand in Hindi. I also studied Swami Dayanand's Satyarath Prakash. I was very impressed by his views on reforms, but could not appreciate the chapter where he criticized all the other religions. At this time came an English book called *'Mother India'* by a Miss Mayo, in which she depicted Indians as characterless, lazy, liars, who could not be trusted. Besides all this she harped on some of the customs that the educated Indians themselves were keen to rectify. Lala Lajpat Rai as an answer wrote *"Unhappy India"* which took the whole of India by storm. This book was written in the late twenties, but I read it much later.

This was the time when the Prince of Wales of England wanted to marry Wallis Simpson who was already divorced twice. Their romance became the favourite subject of teenagers who almost worshipped him like a hero. Here was a man ready to give up his throne to marry the woman he loved. I would read every thing that appeared in the press and felt quite sympathetic towards them, then one day one of the girls said *"He has shown more guts than Shri Rama, who gave up a chaste wife Sita for the sake of the kingdom, and here is a man who is ready to abdicate his throne for his beloved"*. Most unconsciously came my answer. *"Please don't compare him with Shri Rama, he gave up his wife and also his own happiness for he sincerely loved Sita, because he put his duty before everything else"*. It became clear to me that selfish love was not the be-all and end-all of life. However I sincerely hoped that

INDIAN SPRING

the Prince of Wales would never regret his decision and would lead a happy life. But he was unhappy that his family seemed very unkind and unfair by never accepting his wife as a part of the family. After a lapse of nearly seventy years, a similar situation again arose in Britain early in 2005. Charles, Prince of Wales and heir to the throne, a divorcé himself with two sons married another divorcée with two children. People have accepted the marriage, the only condition being that his wife Camilla will not be called the Queen but Princess Consort.

After my matriculation, as the Diocesan College had closed I joined a new college, the Ashutosh College, which held classes for girls from 7.00 am to 10.30 am and then for boys from 11.00 am onwards. Mother liked the idea very much as I would be with her the whole day. As the days were rather long, I took up a little knitting and embroidery, besides reading.

In the intermediate examination I won a scholarship for entrance to University. I got Rs. 20 a month for two years and could choose any College without paying any fees. I should really have joined the Scottish Church College, which had just turned into a co-ed institution and was considered the best, even better than the Presidency College which had the best staff. But I continued in the Ashutosh College because it was near and convenient. Mother would say *"If she has done well in her intermediate, she will do well in her BA also, she is not appearing for the Indian Civil Service (ICS) that we should be so particular".* And I did do quite well in my BA also.

For my MA there was no choice. I either had to give up studies or go to the University which was co-educational. The University was right in the heart of the city at least 10 km away from our house. I had never done such a long distance by bus or tram, and studying with boys was also something new. My parents must have realized that I was quite nervous. Father insisted that I always went by a chauffeur-driven car, and that the car would wait till I finished my classes. I was pleasantly surprised to find the boys were very well behaved. There was a special ladies room, where the girls could sit and chat if they did not want to go to the library. An assistant would knock at the door to indicate that the professor had arrived in class and then the girls would walk in. Once the lecture was over the professor would wait for the girls to leave before he left. In a class of a hundred boys, we were four girls.

Till the time I did my BA I thought I knew a lot and felt quite happy and proud about the knowledge I had gained. In my MA I realized that I knew very little. I had never seen such a big library where I was expected to study on my own. I felt like a frog from a well, thrown into an ocean and left to swim. I suddenly found it very difficult. I then wished I had joined the Scottish Church College. It perhaps would have served as a better stepping stone to the University.

Occasional debates were held and I particularly remember one. Sir S. Radhakrishnan was conducting it and was the judge. We were given five minutes to speak and then the bell would ring indicating us to stop. I spoke very nicely for about four minutes and suddenly I found myself going blank and tongue-tied. Sir Radhakrishnan waited a few seconds. He must have realized that I would not be able to continue and he rang the bell. Most spontaneously I said with a wide smile *"Thank you Sir for coming to my rescue"*. There was a hearty applause and later in his remarks Sir Radhakrishnan said that I had the making of a good speaker. It was a compliment I never forgot. Sir Radhakrishnan later became President of India.

On Holidays and Travels

Besides going to Darjeeling every year for the summer vacation, my most memorable holiday came in 1936, when my parents decided to travel abroad. The choice was between going to Europe or a visit to Burma, Singapore, China and Japan. After a lot of thought the choice fell on Japan. It was decided that I would accompany my parents because I was of an age when it could be beneficial for me from an educational point of view. Nirmala was too young and could stay back with my brothers.

We sailed in a small ship and felt quite seasick for the first twenty-four hours. I became quite apprehensive that if the whole trip was going to be like that it would be a complete disaster. We were very thankful to see land again and were in Rangoon, where we stayed for three days with the agent of the Central Bank. We were very well looked after and did a lot of sightseeing, particularly the Buddhist Pagodas. From there we went on a bigger ship and reached Singapore. In Singapore, we were received by a Punjabi family. We stayed in one of the best hotels in the heart of the city which arranged our sight seeing programme. What impressed me most was the cleanliness of the city and the lovely roads, for we did a lot of driving. From Singapore we got into a luxury liner of the P & O, their best ship called the S.S Rawalpindi. Visits to Hong Kong and Shanghai were from the ship, which anchored for a couple of days in each place. The journey on the ship was most enjoyable. It was like living in a five star hotel, with excellent food, comfortable cabins and beautiful lounges. There was dancing, and swimming. Although we did not participate in all the activities, it was most enjoyable to watch. We had a Goanese butler serving our table and he would very sweetly suggest the dishes we would like. Mother loved asparagus, and we had a lot of fish and chicken with Russian salad.

Once we landed in Japan, we took a conducted tour of about 12 days. We were shown several towns, which involved a lot of sightseeing. We attended a Japanese tea party, which was full of bows and rituals. We went to a late night Geisha Dance which was very colourful, with lanterns and fans. We saw lots of Buddhist temples and gardens; after all, we were visiting the land of cherry blossoms and chrysanthemums.

INDIAN SPRING

We were very impressed by the 10 penny stores where hundreds of items lay and we could pick up anything and pay at the counter. It was something very new for us, for we were used to asking the price of each item and then try to get the price reduced. It was the first time that we saw escalators, and felt quite excited and nervous getting on to them, but I have always found them a little inconvenient because the saree can easily get stuck. Mother did a little shopping in China of house linen with Chinese embroidery and silk, but she felt very disappointed that she was not able to buy any sarees, as the material in the shops had a width of 36 inches, whereas for sarees, 45 inches was required. The last two days were in Yokohama from where we were to board our ship again for our return journey.

Father had a letter of introduction to a Sindhi family who had a branch in Yokohama. Father rang them up and they asked us to come to their wholesale shop. We reached there at about 10 am. Here Mother found all she was looking for and hearing the prices, she just went on setting aside sarees, velvets, crepes, curtains, quilt materials. After a while Father, reminded her that we were going sightseeing at 11 am. *"Let us miss the morning tour "*. The following day, she insisted on having one more trip to the shop. The shop was used to packing and they put everything into two boxes which were quite light but secure. Once we were on the ship, Mother was quite keen to get back home. Our original plan was to go to Colombo and then South India before returning. Father also felt that we had collected so much luggage that more overland travelling would be quite inconvenient.

So Mother and I returned by ship from Singapore to Calcutta, and Father proceeded to Colombo. Father had wired to my brother that he should be at the jetty to receive us with a fair amount of cash for paying the customs duty.

When we arrived in Calcutta, the ship was anchored mid-stream in the river Hoogly. We had been given a printed proforma on which we were to fill in all the things that were dutiable. Mother could not write English and when I volunteered she told me not to do so. When the customs officers came to our cabin and enquired what we had, Mother said, *"I have got a lot of things, I have a large family and I have presents for everybody, but nothing is for sale"*. One officer looked at the other and they seemed a little uncertain. She said *"Here are the keys, you can see for yourself"*. One of the officers folded his hands and said *"Mataji, koi zarurat nahin"*[24], and we walked out without paying anything. The rule was that no duty was to be charged on things which were for personal use.

Our next important holiday was in May 1940 when Father, Mother, Nirmala and I went to Kashmir. We visited Srinagar where we stayed with Dr. Mathura Das, the famous eye specialist, who was very well known for performing cataract operations. He had a beautiful house on Gupkar road, the most fashionable area of Srinagar. I still remember the rows of cherry, plum and pear trees in their garden. I don't need to describe the beauty of Kashmir. After a wonderful time with picnics, visits to the Shalimar and Nishad Gardens and Chashmeshahi, and *Shikara*[25] rides on the Dal Lake, we visited Gulmarg for a couple of days. Then to Pahalgam, where we had rented a bungalow near a stream. On reaching Pahalgam, we realized that the pilgrimage to Amarnath was not very far. It was about 28 miles, which could be covered in 3 or 4 days. Mother was quite keen, but Father was a bit hesitant. The journey was not easy. We would have to ride and the altitude was also a deterrent, for people did get palpitations, and if it rained things became difficult for there were no places where we could take shelter. While we were toying with the idea, General and Mrs. Goel came to Pahalgam, and they also seemed quite keen to make the pilgrimage to Amarnath. General Goel was a doctor, and once they had become enthusiastic, Mother said *"Now we have nothing to worry about: a doctor is with us"*. Mother, who was quite heavy, could not ride a horse, so a *dandee*[26], which meant four people would carry her, was arranged. When the coolies saw her they insisted that she would require six coolies because she was so heavy. So we were six people going and we had four horses with four *ghorewalas*[27], two mules with food, and ten dandeewalas[28]. In short we were six, and we had sixteen sherpas to guide us. It was the most exciting trip of my life. Going through snow clad mountains, for miles and miles there was no soul visible. The path was sometimes visible and sometimes the ghorewalas would just take us through narrow gorges. After spending a night at Chandanwari and then at Shesh Nag, the journey was a bit more difficult, we all had back aches but nobody was ready to own up, because we now wanted to complete the journey. There we saw the beautiful lake from a distance, a dark blue colour, which is unforgettable. The following day we reached Panchtarni, which made the seniors including the General a little breathless. He was carrying some medicines and gave something to his wife and to Mother so that they would have a comfortable night. Next morning we woke up very early to be able to have the *Darshan*[29] of the *Lingam*[30], which is ice. We saw it from a distance, and did our *Pranam*[31]. It was extremely cold, and so we started on the return journey. We were able to reach Chandanwari by 5 pm. The ghorewalas were quite keen to bring us back, but we insisted on spending the night there as we were very tired. Early next morning, we returned to Pahalgam. We would have liked to take it easy, but the coolies were keen to get back, as they would be able to earn an extra day's income. This was the first and last pilgrimage I had with my parents, and undoubtedly the most difficult one.

How times have changed! We were six people, two fairly old men, two middle-aged ladies who could just about walk, and two young girls, and we had sixteen Muslim coolies who were guiding us. To all intents and purposes, we had trusted our lives to them. In the four days not for a minute did we have any sense of fear. They treated us with great respect and saw to our comforts.

Today we would suspect them, and think twice before undertaking such a hazardous journey without proper guards. With terrorism prevailing and the Kashmir issue unresolved, I don't think anyone would venture a trip today like the one we had, in spite of so much security. A bomb blast on the pilgrims seems to be a normal routine. Only the other day, I read about the attack on the Amarnath pilgrims in July 2003, when thousands of pilgrims had to abandon their visit to the holy shrine.

My Brothers and Sisters

Before I get to the subject of my marriage, I must devote a small chapter to my brothers and sisters.

My eldest brother, Som Prakash, was held in great respect. When we shifted to Calcutta he stayed in Lahore to complete his schooling. He was studious and hardworking, a year ahead for his age. After his matriculation he joined the Government College, Lahore and came home only for his vacations. He graduated at the age of nineteen and went to England to study banking. He worked with the Midland Bank for a small stipend. He was supported by father, and did his Banking Institute exams. He returned after three and a half years, enrolled as an officer with the Imperial Bank of India, which was later known as the State Bank of India. It was an excellent job and soon after his arrival he got married to Kunti, daughter of Sir Ram Nath Chopra. The Puris and Chopras were known to each other and were very good friends. In fact, Brother was the only member who knew them less as he was in Punjab most of the time. Kuntibibi was a very talented girl, painting and sculpture were her hobbies. She was very well read and ran a very good home. Their son Arjun was born in 1934, and was the first grandchild of the Puri family and has always had a very special place because he was a very lovely and an affectionate child, and has always shown a very special care for his uncles, aunts, and cousins.

My second brother, Sukh Dev Prakash, popularly known as Devji, was born ten months after my eldest brother. His birth was premature, and he needed a lot of care. The third brother, Sarup Prakash, arrived after fifteen months, a strong robust baby. These two were brought up like twins. Devji's schooling was withheld for a year and these two brothers started schooling together. They were now three years behind Somji. They did their intermediate together. Devji did not want to study any further and wanted to get into business. He first joined the Bedis but that did not work out. He then joined the Sunlight India Insurance Company which was started by our cousins in Lahore. Sarupji proceeded to England to study banking and came back with the same qualifications as the eldest brother. The Imperial Bank had stopped direct recruitment from England and he joined the Reserve Bank, which had just started.

Devji got married to Kamla, daughter of Mr. Sant Ram, who was a district magistrate. This was an arranged marriage, on the recommendation of our cousins in Lahore. Only pictures were exchanged. Kamlabibi made a very good wife and daughter-in-law. She was a lovely girl with very good values. Six months after Devji's marriage Sarupji got married to Lalo: a pet name that stuck to her. She was the daughter of Mr. Manoharlal who was Advocate-General in Patna, and later became the Judge of the Patna High Court. Sarupji and I went to Mussoorie to meet them. She was a very capable girl, very fond of music and full of life.

Shaktiji after his matriculation went to the Government College Lahore and came back after his intermediate. On account of a little ill health, he was advised to live in a healthier climate and he settled down in Darjeeling. He got married to Savitri, daughter of Mr. Shiv Ram Bhasin who was practicing law in Ferozepore. Her brother, Dev Raj, and my eldest brother were friends in England. Dev Raj came to Calcutta and stayed with us looking for a suitable job. He recommended his sister as a suitable bride for Shaktiji. Savitri was a good-looking woman who showed a lot of business acumen, and had an ice-cream business which was very successful. My sister Sarla was younger than all the brothers, but she got married soon after Somji's wedding at the age of eighteen and a half to K.C. Khosla, a qualified Civil Engineer from Edinburgh. She was a very quiet girl with a lot of art and music in her. She went into marriage with the idea of making an ideal wife. She had only seen the eldest brother doting on his wife. She had never seen or heard Father raising his voice at Mother. So she went into marriage with lovely dreams and found reality a little different, as we all do. Her husband was exacting and adjustments were fairly difficult. Slowly and steadily things improved, and she became a very successful wife and an excellent mother to four children who doted on her. Life can take such a turn that when her husband died at the age of 90, her only regret was that God did not grant her earnest desire to die before her husband, such was the attachment.

Why I have written all this is because her marriage had a profound effect on me. It never occurred to me that I should just not get married, but I was determined that I would never bring my troubles to my parents. I would never allow my husband to impose his will on me, and I would never be afraid of him.

My younger sister Nirmala got married six months after me to Harkrishen Kapur, son of a businessman Ram Jawaya Kapur of Lahore. They had a very successful printing business and H.K. worked with his Father, having a luxurious life style.

As years went by, there was more contact between the brothers. Two of them were living in Calcutta, the brother from Darjeeling always spent the winter months in Calcutta, and even my eldest brother was posted there a number of times. Sarlabibi's husband was also posted there. I was away and so was Nirmala. Later on, when my husband was in Air Headquarters, we were together with Sarlabibi, and had a lot of contact with Nirmala also, as her family shifted to Delhi after Partition. So the sisters were more in touch with each other. Much later, after Father's death, Devji shifted to Agra where Nirmala and H.K. were already established. So we met Devji and his family much more. After my eldest brother retired and bought a farm in Chattarpur, on the outskirts of Delhi, we had very close contact with both of them. After my sister-in-law Kuntibibi passed away, I made it a point to visit him regularly and spend time with him. I always treated him as a father figure and received a lot of affection from him.

After all the four brothers and Sarlabibi were married, Nirmala and I had a lot of companionship. She was four years younger. We looked very different. She was tall, dark and heavy, while I was very thin and much shorter than her. Our interests and tastes were also different. I was interested in books; she was more into fun and games, dancing and music. She did not have much formal training in music, but had an extremely powerful voice and could pick up tunes without any effort. She loved non-vegetarian food, while I was not a great connoisseur of food. Our biggest problem arose when we were going to bed. We had to share the bedroom. She wanted the fan full speed, while I wanted it much slower. I wanted to read in bed before sleeping, and she wanted the lights off, for she was quite tired after hectic activity during the day. More often than not she got her way, because Mother would generally side with her and say *"She is your younger sister, let her have the fan, you can use a light blanket"*. In spite of these differences, we were very fond of each other and later on in life also we were great pals. She always respected me and I never underestimated her intelligence and views on any subject, and generally we thought alike.

My Marriage

After appearing for my MA examination in 1941, I went to Bangalore with Maluk Singhji. The Bedis had procured a big contract for building an aerodrome, and Pushpabibi and the whole family were there. My parents and Nirmala also came after a couple of weeks. On their way in Madras, they met my husband-to-be, who was then invited to Bangalore where he could meet me. There had obviously been some correspondence between my Father and him of which I was not aware. But his Father had written to him to meet me and if he approved, the marriage could be arranged as he was quite satisfied about the family.

He arrived in a Ford sports car, with his bearer, and stayed with us for about four days. He was an aeronautical engineer, qualified from de Havilland in Hatfield, England, and was now working as Chief Engineer for the Madras Flying Club. I found him pleasant, with pleasing manners, and though he was very dark, he had a very good personality.

During the four days with us he told me about his family. His father, Dewan Durga Prasad, was a leading lawyer in Ferozepore. They originally came from Kunjah, a small town near Gujrat. His mother, Pratap Kaur came from the Gurus Sodhi family of Guruharsahai. He had two older sisters, both married to lawyers, well settled with children. His two older brothers had also qualified from England. The elder, Ram Prasad (popularly know as Raja), an aeronautical engineer, was married to Chand, daughter of an eminent lawyer of Montgomery. Krishna Prasad, the second brother, a veterinary surgeon with the Army, was married to Rajan, a Sikh girl from Attari but brought up by the Maharaja of Jind.

My husband's name was Narinjan Prasad Nair, and I will now refer to him as N.P. That is how I always addressed him, as it was not customary to call one's husband by his first name, just as even now people never address their parents by their first names. I used to call my Mother and Father Bhaboji and Bauji. My husband addressed his parents as Maji and Dewan Sahib. "Ji" is generally added to a name to show respect.

Our marriage was fixed for 27 September, during *Navratras*[32], which is considered a very auspicious time.

Father gave Rs.100 to N. P. as *Shagan*[33], and another Rs. 500 for his Father. On reaching Ferozepore, he sent a parcel for me consisting of a beautiful Benares sari, and a diamond ring. No big fuss was made about the engagement, as is done by the rich these days by having big functions of *Thaka*[34] and then *Shagan* before the wedding.

N.P. took a month's leave from 14 September and went to Ferozepore. It is customary for the boy's people to go to the bride's home for the marriage ceremony with their friends and relations, and they would be entertained by the bride's side. My father-in-law agreed to have the wedding in Calcutta and decided to bring only four people: he himself, N. P., and his two sons-in-law. N. P.'s elder brother was posted in Calcutta and the other brother who was a Captain in the Army was posted in a non-family station and was not able to come. It was also customary to have the *Barat*[35] of only men folk, so the question of any ladies joining the *Barat* did not arise. The modern trend is very different for there are many women singing and dancing on the road, making it a big *tamasha*. Then a marriage was considered a far more serious, formal and a dignified function where every one was expected to be on their best behaviour. As the journey to Calcutta was long and tedious my father-in-law wanted to spend an extra day in Calcutta, so that he was fully rested before the wedding. In view of the long journey back, Father thought that it was a very reasonable request, and considering that the bridegroom's party was so small, readily agreed. The *Barat* was put up in the palatial bungalow of the Bedis, who were in Bangalore.

The *Barat* was received by my brothers and some of Father's friends. It was customary for the fathers to meet at the time of Milni (exchange of garlands) when the bridegroom is at the bride's house. A hearty breakfast and lunch were laid for them. In the evening, they indicated that they wanted whisky when soft drinks were brought in. My brother Sarupji, who was deputed to look after them, rang up Father and told him. Father just said *"Please tell them that I don't serve whisky to my guests"*. Sarupji took N.P. aside, pointing out that Father never served whisky as a matter of principle. N.P. then said that he would like to go out for dinner somewhere and Sodhi Sahib said that he had after all came to Calcutta to enjoy and see a little bit of night life. They wanted to ring for a taxi, but brother put a car at their disposal. They both went to some restaurant and let the driver off. They came back at midnight and found my brother waiting for them. Next day Father arranged a lavish lunch for them at the Great Eastern Hotel, where they could have ordered any amount of drinks. Much to my brother's relief they ordered only soft drinks. In the evening, they arrived in time where all our guests were present. A lovely tea was laid for about 500 people and everything passed off nicely. I was kept in the dark about the whole incident. The following day after lunch was the *Doli*[36] and we went to Raja Bhai Sahib's house and later to the station as the train did not leave till 8.30 p.m. In the car the first words that N.P said to me were *"I didn't want any misunderstanding. I meant no offence to your brother or the family'.* Since I knew nothing, I just kept quiet, and he did not elaborate any further. But I was quite worried, and at the station I took my brother aside and told him what N.P. had said. My brother just embraced me and said. *"I am glad that he said so, I think he is a gentleman".*

Now when I think about the incident I feel that perhaps my family made a mountain out of a mole hill, but at that time, sixty-four years ago, I can well imagine the anxiety my parents must have gone through and how apprehensive they must have been about N.P.'s drinking habits.

I found N.P. very kind and considerate. We reached Lahore and spent a few hours with Rajan, N.P.'s elder brother's wife, and proceeded to Ferozepore by car where my mother-in-law and sister-in-law Prakashvati were eagerly awaiting us. My eldest sister-in-law had just had a baby son and was not able to come. I found Maji extremely good-looking but frail, very pleasant, and considerate, Behanji was also very affectionate, but I could see that for them their father was the dominating figure and the pivot of the entire household. After staying in Ferozepore for three days, we went to Lahore for four days, before proceeding to Calcutta. It was customary for the newly-wed couple to return to the bride's house, more as reassurance to the bride's parents that all was well, before settling down to routine life.

While in Lahore, where I had several relatives, I could not make up my mind whether I should visit them. As we were driving through I saw the house of one of my cousins, Dr. Maharaj Krishan Kapur. I told N.P. to stop the car and said *"Let us see them for a few minutes"*. He readily agreed, and we were heartily welcomed. I told my cousins that since we were in Lahore for just another two days it would not be possible for us to meet all the relations. *"You both come for tea tomorrow, and I will have them all here"* she said. I looked at N.P. He did not say anything, and I accepted the invitation. She patted N.P. and said *"See you tomorrow"*, and he said *'Yes'* with a smile. The following day after our afternoon nap, we were sitting with Rajan and N.P. said *"I am feeling quite lazy I didn't feel like changing"*.

Rajan's prompt reply was *"Don't go"* I looked at both of them very surprised and she continued *"and who wants to meet relatives when one is newly married"*. I was a little worked up by then, and I retorted *"Is he the only one who is newly married? I have done nothing but be with his relatives for the last six days and even now I am sitting with you. It will do him no harm if he meets mine for a few minutes. I am getting ready and I would like to leave in twenty minutes"*. and left the room. I was now shivering in my shoes that what will be my next move if he does not get ready. After about five minutes, he came in and we both went to the party. Rajan had been invited but she declined. I must add that Rajan was striking to look at and very fond of children and animals.

It was a lovely party and all my relations had brought presents and it was a very pleasant evening. On our return in the car he said *"I am glad that we came"*. I just kept quiet, but felt happy that I had been able to assert myself. When we reached Calcutta, after meeting me, my parents felt a little reassured and happy. My only regret was that they had seen anxiety and worry about my happiness even before I was married. After staying in Calcutta for a couple of days, we were again travelling on a long journey to Madras. Fortunately, we were always able to get a coupé and that was the only time we had to ourselves. We spent about a 100 hours in the train, which in a way was a blessing in disguise as it gave us ample time to talk and get to know each other.

NARINJAN PRASAD NAIR AND BASANT
AFTER THEIR WEDDING, CALCUTTA 1941

AIR COMMODORE N.P. NAIR, 1964

Narinjan and Basant, Patiala Club, 1970

During the journey he told me more about his childhood. His father married off the two elder daughters while they were in the teens and had done a little schooling. He was very keen to give his sons the best education. He thought that the schools of Ferozepore did not have a very good standard, so he sent the two elder boys to Colonel Brown's school in Dehra Dun. After that he still had to find careers for them, so he decided to send the youngest son N.P. to the Royal Indian Military College (RIMC), so that after passing out from there he would automatically get a commission in the Indian Army. Entry to the RIMC was quite difficult. The Governor of the province to which the child belonged interviewed him before he was admitted and the fees were quite high. N.P. went there at the age of thirteen. After six years, the day before he was to be commissioned, he was declared medically unfit for a very minor defect in his left ear. The disappointment for him and his parents was intense. He was now over nineteen, and the colleges did not recognize him as a graduate. So he went to first year college, but he was so frustrated that he left studies. He said he wanted to work, but he was not really qualified for any special vocation. He got a small job as a mechanic in the Indian National Airways, where his brother was holding an excellent position as an aeronautical engineer in the officer's grade. After spending a few months there he returned to Ferozepore and told his parents that he wanted to go to England for aeronautical training also. His father was very reluctant for he said he had spent enough money on him at RIMC. This was one occasion when his mother took a firm stand and insisted that he should be given a chance to qualify, for the child could not be blamed if he was declared medically unfit for the army. So he ultimately went to England, returned as a qualified engineer and was holding the job of chief engineer of the Madras Flying Club when I married him.

As a bachelor, N.P. was staying in a boarding house as a paying guest in one of the best localities of Madras. The accommodation was a small cottage, a drawing room, bedroom, and a toilet. We were expected to eat in the common dining room. It was very comfortable but I wanted a home, a place of my own. Very soon we found a bungalow, near the airport which was his work place. His hours were quite odd. He left at about 6.30 am, returned for lunch at about one o'clock and went back to the airport again for a couple of hours in the evening at about 5.00 pm.

He was full of life, ready to go for a drive, to a restaurant, or a dance evening on a Saturday night, or even a late show cinema. He was ever ready to spend on food or entertainment and never counted his pennies.

In setting up the household, I employed a cook and bearer, and later an ayah.

Since N.P.'s eldest brother did not have any children (on account of my sister-in-law's ill health), N.P. was keen to have a baby as soon as possible, and within four months of my marriage I realized that I was becoming a mother.

The War Years

The World War had begun in 1939, but initially India was not affected very much. In December 1941, when the Pearl Harbour incident took place, America joined the war. Japan was siding with Germany. There was now a prospect of Calcutta and Madras becoming the target of bombing. One day N.P. came home and told me that he had received three months' notice terminating his services, as the Club had to close down because the aerodrome was to be made available to the military. I was naturally very upset and did not have the heart to inform my parents. I took up a brave stand and told him that I really did not like this job at all, because he was already at the top and had no further prospects. Surely he did not want to spend all his life in a flying club with no further promotion, and here was an opportunity to look for something better. At that time, the Royal Air Force (RAF) threw open the technical branch to Indians. A senior officer of the RAF had come to Madras to see what kind of aircraft could land there. He met N.P. and asked him to apply for an officer's job in the technical branch. N.P. immediately did so. However, within a fortnight he came home smiling that the Flying Club had withdrawn the notice and all was well.

One Sunday morning we went to Adiyar, which was famous for its gardens and housed the Theosophical Society, which was very active. I knew about it as the famous Annie Besant was the founder member. On roaming around the building I saw a notice board, which indicated that Madame Montessori, the famous Italian educationalist who specialized in child development, was going to conduct a three months' course, and applications were invited. She had come to India for a short while, but was interned indefinitely when Italy joined the war against Britain. So the British now kept her in Adiyar, knowing that she was a great educationalist, she was left in the best surroundings and instead of just wasting her time, she volunteered to conduct these classes. I showed a keen interest in the programme and N.P. readily agreed. So I was one of the direct pupils of Madame Montessori, who spoke in Italian while her nephew would translate sentence-by-sentence, and then we were handed over printed copies of the lectures. Besides that, practical classes were held where the Montessori toys were presented and games introduced to hold the interest of the children, and at the same time the children were really being taught. She laid great stress on children observing nature and being made aware of natural beauty. I now feel a little sad that some modern parents lay a lot of stress only on the quality of the furniture and toys, which may not have any great influence on the children who seem to want constant change to get rid of boredom.

The war was on and by February 1942, things were getting hot and people were thinking of evacuation as Madras was considered very vulnerable. My sister Nirmala's marriage was fixed for April 1942, and N.P. wanted me to go to Delhi for sometime and stay with his brother Raja Bhai Sahib and his wife before proceeding to Lahore for the wedding. So I went to Delhi, where Raja Bhai Sahib and Chandji gave me a lot of affection and care, and I really enjoyed being with them. While in Delhi I realized that I was pregnant. I then went to Ferozepore for a few days. Maji was very sweet and had a charming personality and did her best to make me comfortable. She also mentioned that whenever I have a son, she would like him to be called either Om or Pratap. She came to Lahore to attend Nirmala's wedding so that she would get some idea how our wedding must have been celebrated. She was very happy to meet my parents. That was the last time I saw her. After Nirmala's wedding, I insisted on returning to Madras to be with my husband.

Our child was due at the end of October. In August 1942, *The Quit India* resolution was passed and 8 August was chosen as the direct action day by the Congress. A day before, all the leaders were arrested. All hell was let loose on 8 August. The masses just became violent, and there was complete chaos, with government property being destroyed. The railway system broke down completely. It took months for conditions to normalize. There was no question of my leaving Madras and my mother-in-law promised to come to us for my delivery. Unfortunately, while in Delhi she had a nasty fall and fractured her wrist. She decided to return to Ferozepore, where she died on 16 October 1942 just about a couple of weeks before my child was to be born. My parents were informed of her death, and now my Mother insisted that one of the family members should be with me for the confinement. My sister Sarlabibi arrived just three days before my son was born and we called him "Om" which was my mother-in-law's choice. N.P. did not attend his mother's funeral because Raja Bhai Sahib insisted that I could not be left by myself, and in any case he could not reach there in time for the funeral. The journey to Ferozepore took well over 72 hours.

Om was a lovely baby with very bright eyes and not at all troublesome. When he was about two months' old, N.P. received an interview call from the Royal Air Force and was selected. At this stage, he could either accept or refuse the offer. It was an extremely difficult choice; the war was very much in the eastern sector. He naturally sought my opinion. I was clear on only one point; that the flying club job was just a *tamasha*. At the age of 27 one should be at the bottom of the ladder and climb up to a much bigger height as time went by. He was at the top with no further prospects. However I did not insist that he should join the Air Force, for I was naturally hesitant because of the war. He decided to join, as his was a ground job, and the chances of his going into action were remote.

This meant closing up the house as he was going to Karachi for three months' training. The Bedis were in Bangalore and N.P. left me with them. I wanted to go to Calcutta whenever I found some one going. Travelling and undertaking a 72 hours' journey with a small child alone was unheard of. Pushpabibi and the rest of the family were very hospitable and I felt quite at home with them. Maluk Singhji gave a pet name to my baby and called him "Jugnoo", a little fire fly whose eyes would always shine with every bright smile that he was willing to give us all. I was having a nice time with them when I received a letter from Father that Mother was a little unwell. I realized that she must be quite ill, otherwise Father would not have mentioned her illness, and I left for Calcutta within a few days. That was at the end of January 1943.

My Most Difficult Days

When I reached Calcutta, I was very relieved to find Mother moving about. She had undergone an operation in December 1941 when I visited her also. She was perfectly alright for Nirmala's wedding in April 1942. In January 1943, during a routine check up, the doctors found that the malignancy had reappeared and she needed intensive treatment. She was undergoing the deep X-Ray treatments but to no effect. Her pain and discomfort went on increasing, and the last time she went out of her own accord was on 13 April to a Gurudwara to celebrate Baisakhi, the Punjabi New Year. The doctors then advised radium treatment, which was available in Patna, and we went there. I took Jugnoo with me, and stayed with my sister-in-law Lalo's parents. We spent a couple of weeks there and returned to Calcutta with hardly any improvement. The only place where she could now be treated was the Tata Cancer Hospital in Bombay, which was the best, and a new hospital. There was a lot of correspondence between the doctors who were treating her in Calcutta and the Bombay doctors who said that she should be brought to Bombay for treatment. All possible arrangements were made. Father and his brother who had come from Lahore on hearing of Mother's illness, my baby and I with two servants went to Bombay. We were received by a doctor from the hospital, a few bank officials and Father's friend, a Mr. Khanna. I was to stay with the Khanna's who were living in a flat on Marine Drive. We had a very comfortable journey. Mother, who was mentally very strong, did not complain at all during the journey. On arrival at the hospital she was given a morphine injection to enable her to have a good rest. We did not want to interfere but the following day I found her quite drowsy. On examining her, the doctors told Father that nothing more could be done for her, we could return home, and make it as comfortable as possible for her. On seeing Mother the next morning, I found that she was not responding to me at all. So I told Father that her condition had deteriorated so much in two days that I was reluctant to undertake the journey without medical assistance. Father immediately asked the hospital to give us either a doctor or a nurse to accompany us. So they provided us with a young nurse with very little experience. At the station there were lots of people to see us off including the doctor from the Bank. He asked the nurse what medicines she was carrying. Her answer was morphine injections and one or two other medicines. He rushed to the nearest chemist shop to give her some more medicines for the heart. The journey was a nightmare. The train was seventeen hours late. When at last we got home, Mother was in a coma and passed away two days later on 9 August 1943, giving enough time to all her children to reach Calcutta in time to see her alive for the last time.

During this time, N.P. had been commissioned in March 1943, and was moving every six weeks with his squadron. He visited me twice whenever he was anywhere near Calcutta. He had to go to Kanchanapara occasionally, which was quite close to Calcutta. To be frank, I did not mind his absence all this time for I was busy with Mother's illness. After her death, I was now desperately keen to join him.

On the 13th day after a death it is customary to feed Brahmins, but Father decided otherwise. There was a famine in Bengal, food was scarce, and the poor were going hungry. He gave a meal of *Kichdi*[37] to anyone who wanted a free meal. It was arranged in a park where hundreds of people could be served. The feeding started at 10 am and went on non-stop till 5 pm. This was the famine, which Amartya Sen refers to, and which left a deep impression on him.

In the first week of September 1943 I received a telegram from N.P. that I should join him immediately. It was from Phaphamau. We had never heard of the place, and with greatest difficulty and research, found that it was the aerodrome of Allahabad. On trying to get a railway ticket we were told the nearest station was Allahabad, and I left within 24 hours. He was at the station to receive me. At the station he said that he was going to England for further training. I was too dazed to comprehend exactly what he was saying. I thought we would go to some quarters that would have been allotted to him. Instead he took me to a beautiful bungalow and I was received by Mrs. Durai, a South Indian lady whose husband was a very senior Railway officer. They lived in this bungalow with three lovely teenage daughters. She welcomed me with a very gracious smile and we walked to the drawing room, where tea was waiting. N.P. then explained that since we were going to be in Allahabad for only 3 or 4 days, Mrs. Durai had insisted that I should not be left by myself in a hotel with a small child. She was aware that I was still mourning and sad from losing my Mother, and now this movement of N.P. was not going to be very pleasant either. On asking N.P. how he came to know them, he mentioned that one of his brother officers Moolgavkar knew them, and was very keen to marry one of the girls. So he used to visit them almost everyday, and brought N.P. along. When Mrs. Durai came to know that I was coming she insisted that I stayed with them. It was a great eye-opener for me to see so much care being given to me and Jugnoo by a person I had never met and all I can say today is that Indians still have an ingrained sense of hospitality which is justifiably famous.

N.P. was given six weeks' leave before reporting at Bombay on 1 November 1943. He was not sure how long the training would last but certainly for six months. We left for Ferozepore once his leave began, for I had not met my father-in-law after Maji's death, and he had not seen Jugnoo. After a few days, we left for Dalhousie where K.P.'s wife Rajan had rented a small bungalow while K.P. was somewhere on the Eastern front. While he was away, N.P. did not want me to go back to Calcutta as I had had a long stay with Father. His suggestion was that I should stay in Dalhousie with my sister-in-law and share the expenses. It would be a good holiday, and the climate would be very beneficial for Dalhousie was a popular Hill station. I was very hesitant to accept this proposal as I found Rajan different in some ways, and unconventional. Even with N.P. around who was being very caring and considerate, I found her behaviour a little casual towards me and I think N.P. was able to notice it without my saying very much. Then one day I told him that if he was not keen on my going to Calcutta, I would rather be with my father-in-law in Ferozepore, and in any case I would like to be with him as long as possible and wanted to accompany him to Bombay. N.P. realized how desperate I was and agreed. Nirmala's sister-in-law, Ram Kumari, was married to a naval officer, a Lieutenant Bhandari, and Nirmala wrote to her that I was going to Bombay for a few days. They sent back a telegram inviting me to stay with them. On arrival in Bombay, N.P. went to a camp to report and I was with Ram Kumari and Charanjit, who were very cordial and affectionate. N.P. would come every evening, not knowing when the ship would leave. This went on for several days and I felt a little embarrassed that my stay with them was now becoming weeks instead of just a few days. The Bedis had now got a big contract in Poona (Pune), and they were coming into Bombay for the races every weekend. The Deccan Queen[38] had just started. They insisted that I spend one weekend with them at the Taj and when N.P. left I should spend a while with them in Poona. That was the first time I had the occasion of staying in this famous hotel. On 1 December, N.P. did not come, and I knew that he had sailed. I then went to Poona with the Bedis. Poona has since been renamed Pune, just as Calcutta is called Kolkata, Bombay is Mumbai, and Madras is Chennai.

Although I was very comfortable and well looked after, I was naturally very disturbed and unhappy. I received a very affectionate letter from my father-in-law inviting me to go to Ferozepore. *"This is your real home, and you are most welcome, besides Rajan is also coming for the winter months as Dalhousie is extremely cold so you will have good company".* After a lot of thought I decided to accept his invitation.

I was never able to be close to Rajan, but I had a very cordial relationship with the children as they grew up, particularly with Vijai and Doreen, the eldest son and daughter-in-law. To this day, I have a lot of love and affection for them and they are now living in Noida. Whenever I am in Delhi, they make it a point to come and see me and send greetings for my birthday, New Year and Diwali.

After Rajan went back to Dalhousie, Chandji, my sister-in-law from Delhi, came to spend a month with us in Ferozepore. She was soft-spoken, kind and considerate, God-fearing and loving. But surprisingly, I found that Dewan Sahib was slightly cold and indifferent to her. Much later, I realized that Chandji's not having a child was a little upsetting for him. She also spoke very highly of my mother-in-law, but did not say very much either in favour or against Dewan Sahib.

I was now looking forward to N.P.'s return. The mail was erratic, sometimes there would be no letter for several weeks and then, suddenly, a dozen letters would arrive together. It now occurred to me that all our stuff had reached Bangalore when we left Madras, but I had told the Bedis to send it to Lahore care of Nirmala. On enquiry from her, she said that not a single parcel had been received and the railways could not give any clues, as she had no papers. Then out of the blue, I received a letter from my uncle from Lahore enclosing a postcard addressed to a Mr. Basant saying that there was a package lying in the lost property office of Railways in his name. On receiving this letter, I rushed to Lahore the same day and went to the lost property office saying that there should be about 20 packages. They said that they were all there. On further enquiry, I found that the address was incomplete so the packages could not be delivered. I then asked them how they got my uncle's address. The officer explained that after waiting for several months they wanted to auction all the items, but on opening one parcel which contained the crockery discovered lots of letters which I had written to N.P. from my uncle's house and signed Basant. So they very kindly sent a postcard addressed to Mr. Basant and Uncle very thoughtfully sent it to me, saying that I was the only Basant he knew. It was a great relief to get back all my things.

By April 1944 I wanted to go to Calcutta to meet Father as I was anxious to meet him and see how he was after my Mother's death. Dewan Sahib also agreed, and I went to Calcutta to find Father not only looking and feeling at peace, but he had found a new mission in life that kept him quite busy. On her last journey to Bombay, Mother had said *"What kind of a metropolitan city is Calcutta where cancer cannot be treated. You are able to spend so much on me.... What about the poor who cannot afford these expensive journeys and hospital expenses"*. After her death, Father met the Chief Minister of Bengal, Dr. B.C. Roy, who was an eminent physician himself, and expressed a desire to donate a certain amount for a cancer hospital to be established. Dr. Roy's response was very positive. He said that Father should try and arrange more donations and when he had collected at least 50% of the money required the Government would contribute the other 50%, and a cancer wing would be established in one of the charitable hospitals. He also put him on to two other doctors who went to well placed companies and business houses to explain. In 1946, the Cancer Wing was inaugurated in the Chittaranjan Seva Sadan.

I was now waiting patiently and eagerly for N.P.'s return when suddenly little Jugnoo was taken ill, and died within two days on 9 August 1944, exactly one year after Mother's death. I was inconsolable. I felt as I was in a rudderless boat and left by myself in a rough sea – not knowing where my destiny would take me, what did the future hold for me? I had lost my mother-in-law, my Mother, and now my son, within less than two years. Where was my husband? Somewhere in England, and the newspapers were only talking of England being bombed, evacuations, rationing, blood and sweat. I had promised myself that I would never bother my parents with my troubles, but my plight was an open book for every one. I think that Father was extremely unhappy and equally helpless. One day as I went to his room I found him weeping in a most uncontrollable manner. I went and said *"Bauji, if God gives me a child within one year, I will never cry for Jugnoo"*. Father just embraced me and said *"God is very kind and merciful"*.

Within a week we received a telegram from N.P. that he had reached Bombay and would be with us on 24 or 25 August 1944. It is impossible to describe the feelings I had when I met him. It was a mixture of joy and happiness one moment, and the next moment, pain and sorrow had the upper hand. The feeling of great relief was the only constant factor and my life turned a new leaf.

I Resume a Normal Life Once Again

After a gap of nearly two years, in 1944 I set up my home once again. N.P. was now posted to Risalpur in the North West Frontier Province and attached to a Royal Air Force unit which had mainly British officers. Besides N.P., there was one other Indian officer who was married. He was a Muslim and his wife observed purdah. So basically I was the only Indian woman on the station, as none of the British officers had their wives with them. We were allotted a beautiful three-bedroom bungalow with a large well-maintained garden.

The British officers were very happy and surprised to meet an Indian lady who was quite conversant with European ways, spoke English and even played bridge. Life once again meant enjoyment and laughter particularly after I conceived Praveen. However, I noticed that N.P. was now drinking more regularly, but I did not make an issue of it as he was attached to a British Unit and was mixing with them all the time.

Praveen was born on 2 August 1945 in Calcutta, and my joy knew no bounds to have a lively baby in my arms once again. The day coincided with Sarlabibi's daughter Kusum's birthday. Kusum was eleven years old, and a lovely birthday party was arranged for her. The party became even more joyous as Praveen's birth was also celebrated with a lot of added happiness. Besides, the end of the war was imminent, and we were all looking forward to resuming a peaceful life once again.

On 8 August 1945, the eastern world was shocked to see the devastation caused by atom bombs dropped on Hiroshima and Nagasaki. This came as a complete surprise as the Japanese were on the point of surrender. Instead of joy and enthusiasm at the war ending, there was a feeling of great sorrow and pain. At the end of the first World War, Woodrow Wilson said that America had joined the war to make the world safe for democracy. After World War II, every country now wanted to have nuclear weapons, and the idea of self protection meant armament. The philosophy became that the best way to maintain peace was to be prepared for war.

After the War, N.P. was now posted as Flight Lieutenant to an Indian squadron, which was moving after every four or five months. I joined him in Kanpur (Uttar Pradesh), and then proceeded to Risalpur (North West Frontier Provinces), to Bhopal (Madhya Pradesh), Kolar (Karnataka), and back to Ambala (Punjab) by April 1947. N.P. held the position of Chief Technical Officer (Ambala) with the rank of Squadron Leader.

Life in the squadron was very different to Ambala. The squadron was led by the Commanding Officer, a Wing Commander married to an English girl. This couple liked to be on their own and not mix with the rest of the officers. Then came N.P., another technical officer who was a flight lieutenant, and another married officer who was very friendly. The other ten officers were all young pilots in their early twenties. The Air Force stations were always 8 or 9 miles away from the towns and we were given barrack accommodation near the airfield. Nobody had private transport and the only means of moving to and fro from their rooms to the office and back were bicycles. We were allowed to take the service transport on payment, which we did very occasionally. So we had to carve out a life for ourselves on the station. The young officers would come over to our house quite often and we would play card games and bridge at least three times a week.

Praveen was the only child on the station and these young officers would make a lot of fuss of her. She very soon recognized them and would give them broad smiles. For her first birthday I would have thrown a party for all the officers, but N.P. discouraged me and said it would make it obligatory for them to bring presents, and he did not want that. So I kept quiet. A big surprise lay in store for us because the officers all turned up at tea time with a lovely birthday cake and some toys for Praveen.

In all the towns that we were posted, none of us knew a soul, so it was like a large family moving together, and I can say that the 20 months that we spent with the squadron were most enjoyable. The young officers proved to be very sincere friends and I always followed their careers with a lot of interest. One of them attained the rank of Air Vice-Marshal, but two of them unfortunately had fatal crashes quite early in life. One of them was married and left behind a young wife and two children, while the other was still a bachelor. Ambala was a big Air Force station with a European commanding the station. There were several married officers we could meet and by joining the Civil Club met a lot of other people also.

Independence and Partition

The Indian National Army, which was set up in Singapore under the leadership of Subhas Bose, had joined the Japanese to fight the British, consisted of Indian prisoners of war. Shah Nawaz, Dhillon, Prem Saigal, Muslim, Sikh, and Hindu officers of the Indian Army who had joined the Indian National Army (INA), were accused of treason and were being tried under a Court Martial. The Court was held in public; Bhule Bhai Desai and Pandit Nehru wore their black coats as defence lawyers. Bhule Bhai Desai's speech will go down in history, the purport of which was that a man fighting for the freedom of his own country cannot be accused of treason, but patriotism. The British by this time were aware that the services of police and defence could not be taken for granted. The three officers were not given the verdict of death, but were cashiered with all the others who joined the Indian National Army. During this time while the war was still on, the papers reported that Subhas Bose died in an air crash. But to this day, people have their doubts and several committees have been appointed to check the details, but no progress has been made and no conclusive proof of his death has been found.

The national movement also got a fresh impetus and a mission was sent to India under the leadership of Sir Stafford Cripps to reach some settlement, but the mission failed. There were communal riots in Bengal in 1946, which led to a lot of unrest. Then Lord Mountbatten came on the scene. Churchill by this time was out, and Attlee was the Prime Minister. Suddenly one morning in July it was announced that India would be partitioned and a new state of Pakistan would be carved out. Both countries would become independent on 15 August. My personal reaction to the news was one of real surprise and disappointment. I was amazed that Gandhiji had agreed when for years he had refused to think of a divided India. Radcliffe was appointed to demarcate the line, which would form Pakistan. Wild guesses were afloat, would Calcutta go to Pakistan? What was going to be the fate of Karachi?

Assurances were given that nothing untoward would happen. Life in both the countries would continue to be the same. The Armed forces were given the choice of joining whichever country they preferred. Being Punjabis, we could have opted for Pakistan, but we did not. In spite of the fact that India was being partitioned there was great jubilation and excitement.

We were in Ambala. A big party was arranged at the Air Force mess to celebrate Independence Day. The Commanding officer was British and he heartily joined and co-operated in all the arrangements. N.P. came home and mentioned that there was a Bengali officer who was very keen to finish the function with a national song, either Vandemataram, composed by Bankim Chatterjee, or a Jana Gana composition of Tagore, but he did not have all the words. I asked N.P. to go and bring him to the house. He was absolutely thrilled to find a Punjabi lady who knew both the words and the tunes of both the songs. We decided to sing Jana Gana Mana, which later on was recognized as the National Anthem.

On the morning of 15 August 1947, the papers were full of the function at the Red Fort in Delhi where Pandit Nehru unfurled the Indian National Flag and gave at midnight his famous speech *"A Tryst with Destiny"*.

The next morning there was whispering news that all was well in India, but Pakistan was creating problems for the Hindus. Within 24 hours, hordes of Hindus were being forced to leave their homes, killings were taking place, houses were being looted, Hindu women were committing suicide to save their honour. Trains full of dead bodies were arriving in Delhi. Then hell broke loose in Delhi and Punjab. There was retaliation on the same scale. The Hindus of Punjab and Muslims of Uttar Pradesh and East Punjab were equally affected. The only difference was that while India had Gandhi to save the Muslims, the Hindus of Pakistan had to run for their lives. Pandit Nehru had to invite Mountbatten back to Delhi to manage affairs, as he had no experience of running a government or any idea how to tackle the situation. The euphoria of freedom was taken over by anxiety and fear. There was no home in East Punjab or Delhi, which was not like a refugee camp. People were pouring in using any mode of transport that was available. If they got nothing, they just walked till they could not walk any more and lay on road sides, grateful if they even got a glass of water. Refugee camps were opened in Amritsar, Jullunder, right up to Delhi. There were hardly any Hindus left in Pakistan, but the Muslims of India particularly South India were mainly unaffected. Only the Muslims of East Punjab and Bengal and U.P. were affected to some extent.

I was in Ambala during Partition and moved to Kanpur soon afterwards, and can speak about the Sikh and Hindu refugees, who showed remarkable courage, grit and self respect. Man, woman, and child were ready to earn an honest living. There were no cases of dacoits or thefts, nobody reverted to beggary. People were ready to make a humble beginning. Women would cook food and the menfolk would sell it on the roadside. Non-vegetarian cuisine of the North West Frontier Province was well known. Very soon the tandoori chicken and fish became very popular. Punjabi vegetarian food also came to the forefront. Thus the Moti Mahal restaurant became famous for its chicken, and Quality restaurants for channa bhaturas and ice cream. People who could not afford to invest very much did not hesitate to sell popcorn or sugarcane juice. In a short time lots of little Dhabas and restaurants came up. Entertaining and eating out came into fashion. Many Punjabi women could knit, and would take orders and knit for hours to be able to earn a little. Sindhi women did excellent embroidery and worked on dresses and saris. In Delhi, a women's committee was set up to help refugee women to sell their products. A small shop was set up on Queensway (now Janpath) called Cottage Industries which became very popular. After a while, the Government helped to add more artifacts from other parts of India. Today it is one of the most sought after shopping precincts of Delhi. People who had property in Lahore were given land in Delhi, thus came up the posh colonies of Golf

Links, Patel Nagar, Friends Colony, Maharani Bagh, and Punjabi Bagh. In fact one can say that today Delhi is dominated by Punjabis. Chandigarh as the capital of Punjab came up later.

Some Unexpected Visitors

Coming back to my own life, after about 10 days N.P. came home to say that some family members of the Royal family of the Nawab of Bhopal, mainly women and children and a few servants, were coming from Simla. They had to spend the night in Ambala, and were to be flown to Bhopal the following morning. Being the senior-most married officer, the Commanding Officer (CO) asked N.P. to put them up for the night and N.P. just said *'alright'*. The instructions had come from Mountbatten's office that arrangements were to be made for their stay. The CO did not want to put them in the Officers Mess, so he asked N.P. I was aghast and completely bewildered. How could I possibly put up Muslims in my house? I was frightened out of my wits. We were just two of us, and little Praveen and one servant, and supposing their servants chose to get violent? There was the other angle also: supposing some Hindu families came to know that we were sheltering a whole lot of Muslims and chose to enter the house? N.P. went back to the Commanding Officer and pointed out that we could not possibly provide so many beddings and food to so many people, but did not say that I was very frightened also. The CO just said that he would arrange to send some bedding and food. When they arrived I locked myself in my room and let the mess servants feed them. They were shown the two bedrooms I had prepared for them.

Early next morning the mess servant did not arrive. My sense of hospitality forced me to come out and serve breakfast. They were a perfect lot of ladies with lovely children and very polite servants. It was such a relief to meet them. I realized that if I had a bad night in India in my own home, how could they have had a comfortable night? What mistrust can do!

Within the next three weeks, N.P. received orders to proceed to Kanpur to take over the Aircraft Repair Depot at Chakeri (Kanpur). It was customary for the officer to move by himself and stay in the Mess till he was allotted a house and then the family would join him. I was determined not to be on my own and so we decided that I would go to Delhi and be with Sarlabibi as she had a flat there. Her husband was posted there. Even a train journey to Delhi seemed unsafe. While we were still thinking about our move, Air Commodore Meher Singh came to Ambala and said that the following morning he was flying to Delhi with some civilians. I immediately said *"But civilians are not allowed"*, and he replied *"But sister these are different times; certain civilians cannot take the risk of travelling by train"*. *"In that case, an Air Force wife should also be allowed"*. He answered *"If you can be at the airport by 7 o'clock in the morning. I will take you"*. *"With my bag and baggage?"* I said. *"Yes"*, he replied. We did our packing till early hours of the morning, and reached the airport with Praveen and the Ayah, and all the stuff, which was semi-packed. That was the first and the last time I was ever to be in an Air Force aircraft. N.P. came to Delhi in another plane and we went to Sarlabibi's house to find that Nirmala's father-in-law was also there. He had left his wife and younger son in Amritsar.

During this time my Father, Devji, with his wife and four daughters, Nirmala, H.K. and their son little Madhu were in Kashmir. They thought it was better to extend their stay in Srinagar and return when things settled down, but conditions started getting worse in Kashmir and there was a new danger of Pakistan attacking Kashmir. Father would try to get seats to return to Delhi but found it impossible to get a dozen seats. The transport people would offer him was one or two seats, which he refused for he was not willing to leave the family behind.

At this time Raja Bhai Sahib mentioned that the Indian National Airways had been requisitioned and planes were carrying petrol and equipment to Srinagar, returning empty. Since I had had a ride in an Air Force plane, I asked him if he could bring back my family. The next morning a plane was going, and as an engineer officer he wanted to go, but there was another officer whose wife was also in Srinagar and also wanted to go. However Rajaji gave him my Father's name and address and he promised to ring up and ask him to reach the airport by 3 pm and he would bring them back. Devji received the message and the family did all the packing, got a couple of taxis and loaded the luggage. Only Father was not at home, still trying to get seats and returned home quite exhausted at about 2 pm for lunch to find the family waiting patiently for him. They were certainly not going to leave without him and the drive to the airport took nearly 45 minutes. Rajaji and I were at the aerodrome waiting excitedly and when I saw from a distance Father's turban, tears of joy flowed to see all the family members coming out of the plane.

Partition and how it Affected our Families

As far as my Father's side of the family is concerned, my Father and all my four brothers and elder sister were not affected directly. None of them was in Pakistan and none had any property there. I was affected to the extent that though my father-in-law was in Ferozepore, all his savings were invested in farmlands in Lyallapur, which was considered the granary of India. He was allotted some land in Ambala, which he later sold at a very low price. Thus we were denied a good inheritance. The most affected was Nirmala. Her family left behind a grand style of living for they had a flourishing business in Lahore. Her father-in-law chose to stay on for quite some time until things become impossible. General Kochar (a cousin) arranged to give them a vehicle to put in as much stuff as they could and also themselves, and come out. While staying with Sarlabibi he found a flat right opposite her flat, which was locked, and the Muslim family had migrated to Pakistan. He just opened the lock and walked in. Soon after, Nirmala and H.K. came back from Srinagar. Their story is a story of riches to rags, and back to greater riches. Their better days started when they were allotted land in Golf Links, and they were able to get printing work in Delhi, as well as in Agra where H.K. and Nirmala settled and started printing for the Agra University press. They only left Sujan Singh Park flat after they built their house in Golf Links.

On my husband's side, Dewan Sahib was alright in Ferozepore, and the three brothers were all posted in India and so was Sodhi Sahib's family. Only Prakash Chand Jijaji was in Lahore. Behanji and the children came to Delhi a little before Partition. Only Jijaji (brother-in-law) was in Lahore. The way he was brought out merits attention.

It was almost impossible for Hindus to be seen on the roads with baggage trying to leave and even moving on the streets was dangerous. Two of Chandji's brothers had lost their lives. Planes were going to Lahore but getting to the airport was difficult enough and entry into the airport was almost impossible. There was no way of informing Jijaji that if he could reach the airport, then Raja Bhai Sahib would be able to bring him back. Raja Bhai Sahib, who knew Lahore very well, went with the pilot and requested him to hover around

Jijaji's house. Jijaji on the first day just imagined that it may be Rajaji who is trying to draw his attention, but he put it down to wishful thinking. When the same thing happened the following day, he just left for the airport and was brought back safely. They lost all their possessions, but Jijaji was able to retain his job with the Tatas, who accommodated him in the Delhi office.

Raja Bhai Sahib and Chandji's capacity of helping and caring for others was noteworthy. In a small two-bedroom house on Barber Road, they had at one time, nineteen people living and feeding with them. It was indeed a very difficult time and a great occasion to get to know the real worth of people. Both of them rose to the occasion, earning admiration and gratefulness of all who received help and sympathy.

On the family's arrival, Sarlabibi's flat was also full, but Devji and family left for Calcutta the following day. Father and I left for Kanpur within a week and after that Nirmala and family shifted into a flat opposite. Sarla's husband showed a lot of patience and sympathy and the days we spent with them were as comfortable as possible, under the most distressing conditions.

Family Life after Partition

N.P. was allotted a bungalow soon after he reached Kanpur, so Father and I went to Kanpur and were received by N.P. in his official car; officers were allowed to use an official car by paying a certain amount per mileage done.

Father was absolutely delighted to see the bungalow furnished with Military Engineering Services furniture, and a very well looked-after garden. N.P. had employed a very good cook and a bearer, the beds were made and dinner was ready. Next day N.P. took Father to his office and showed him around the station he was commanding. I could see the thrill written on Father's face to see the size of the station. After six years of my marriage, he saw my home for the first time and he had the satisfaction of knowing and feeling that N.P. was a fine man and I was really well settled.

The house that we were allotted had a drawing room, dining room, two large bedrooms, two attached dressing rooms, four bathrooms, and a guest room. There were six servants' quarters a little away from the main house, which accommodated the cook, bearer, Ayah, a *mali* [39], *dhobi* [40], and the sweeper. The kitchen was on one side of the dining room and had two more small rooms in a row, one for the coal and the last one could be turned into a box room. In front of the porch was the main lawn, and on the side a cemented area which could be used as a badminton court. All around it had permanent plants which were mostly Indian. The famous Indian pink rose which had a beautiful fragrance and could be dried up and used as an essence, the Motia, Java Kusum, Gandh Raj, Rajnigandha[41], Raat ki Rani, and Har Singar for which I do not know the English names. There were creepers like Shantilata and Chameli.

The main lawn had beds around it for annual flowers and when the garden was in full bloom the sight was a riot of colour. The herbaceous border had tall hollyhocks at the back, in the middle came the dahlias, antirrhinums, larkspurs, poppies, phlox, and then the nasturtiums and white elysiums as an edging. There would be a whole walk of sweet peas with little strings woven so that every little plant had a place to climb. We enjoyed the garden very much. In winter we would have lunch in the garden, and in summer the sweeper would throw several buckets of water on the cemented ground, chairs would be put out, a table fan with a long wire would be brought and we would have dinner outside with the sweet fragrance of Raat ki Rani [42].

Electricity and gas were not available for cooking. Food had to be cooked either on kerosene stoves, firewood or coal. In our house we used steam coal, though I knew that in my mother-in-law's house, firewood was used. There were of course no electric egg beaters or mixers. I was amazed to see how our cook could turn out perfect cakes, biscuits and meringues by using a sort of baking pan made out of tin which cost about ten rupees. He would put a *tawa* [43] on the coal on which he would put the cake mixture which he had made using a fork, cover it with the baking pan, and put some live charcoal on it. I really do not know how he was able to control the heat, or how he turned the whole thing, but the dish came out absolutely perfect. Today when I say this to my grandchildren they have a good laugh. They think it is just one of my favourite stories. How can one bake without an oven or a thermostat, a time control, or a microwave?

Although N.P. was not a pilot, he did have to travel by air occasionally if an aircraft could not be brought to the base. One day, it was 30 January 1948, he left in the morning and told me that he would return in the evening. I was walking in our garden and waiting for him when an Air officer walked in with a very sad face. On seeing me, he started weeping and said *"Bhabiji very bad news"*. In that second I thought N.P. must have had a crash but I mustered up enough courage and said *"What has happened?"*, *"Mahatmaji has been shot dead"*. I must admit that my first reaction was one of relief: N.P. is all right. Then the real implications of Gandhiji's death dawned on me. We tuned in to the radio and heard Nehruji saying, *"A Light has gone out of our Lives"*, or words to that effect. Then there were fears: what if a Punjabi Hindu had killed him? How terrible will it be if the Government loses sympathy with the refugees. But it was Nathu Ram Godse from Maharashtra who was caught red-handed. There were no repercussions, not the way Sikhs were treated after Indira Gandhi was assassinated in 1984.

In September 1948, Pavan was born. Chandji and Dewan Sahib were with us, and with his arrival there was a feeling of great joy and happiness. Within a month of his arrival, N.P. was promoted to the rank of Wing Commander with just five years of service. Life was smooth and we made friends with lots of civilians through Mr. and Mrs. Mahendrajit Singh, whom we met with Nirmala's father in-law who was staying with us trying to establish some business. Tosh, as we knew her later, was the daughter of Justice Ram Lal and was a neighbour of Bhapaji (Mr. Ram Jawaya Kapur). She met him in a shop and invited him for dinner and then rang us and invited us also. We liked the couple very much and gradually they became our best friends. Through them we met the entire top society of Kanpur, otherwise we might have been restricted to the Air Force group only.

Praveen went to St Mary's Convent in January 1949, which was right in front of our house. She was hardly three and a half years old. I was quite happy that she enjoyed being in the nursery class. When she was a little over four years old, I was very pleasantly surprised to see the entire English alphabet written across the verandah wall with my lipstick. I was absolutely thrilled and took her in my lap and cuddled her. N.P. was, I think, a little upset to see the whole wall ruined, but when he saw me so happy and excited, he refrained from scolding the child.

The only anxious time we had was when Pavan was about two years old and was bitten by a stray dog which entered our garden. Pavan started walking towards him. I shouted to Pavan to come back but he was bitten before I or the ayah could reach him. He was about the same age as Jugnoo when we lost him. It was very upsetting: the child had to have 14 painful injections and it was heart breaking to see him start crying immediately he heard the noise of the vehicle that the doctor came in.

N.P. was very keen that we should have a dog in the house, so that the children did not have any sense of fear from animals. We were a little unlucky with our first two dogs. We got a Dachshund, a nice clean dog, who was killed when a car ran over him. We then acquired a Pomeranian who died from unknown causes when he was only three months old. After this, for several years, we did not have a dog.

Nirmala and her husband H.K. came to Kanpur to find some partners for a paint factory which H.K. wanted to put up, and spent about six months with us. Nirmala was very fond of flowers and would take a lot of interest in arranging flowers. I saw how much interest the *mali* took watching her and following her directions implicitly, plucking the flowers she wanted very carefully. Later he also made very nice flower arrangements. However there was a guava tree on one side of the garden which caused us a lot of annoyance. Kanpur is famous for its monkey population. The monkey is considered a sacred animal as Hanumanji, who belonged to the monkey clan, had helped Shri

Rama to defeat Ravana and rescue his wife Sita from his clutches. So nobody wants to hurt them, in fact people like feeding them. The guavas attracted the monkeys. They were absolutely unafraid and would jump from one branch to another and quite often ruin other plants. I was quite keen to get rid of the tree but the servants did not like the idea as they were interested in the fruit also.

We had a couple of mango trees which were right at the edge and some branches would be overhanging the road. In the afternoon, when N.P. was away at the office, and the servants were having their afternoon rest, little street urchins would create such a ruction that it was impossible for Nirmala and I to have a nap. I tried to stop them once or twice but Nirmala had another idea. Both of us went outside and asked them if they went to school. One of the bold ones answered. *"There is no school here"*. Nirmala then said *"Alright, if you come here in the morning at 9 o'clock for one hour, we shall teach you to read and write, and also give you a mango each"*.

Next morning, three little boys appeared and we had to keep our word. I gave them some paper and pencils, and put a couple of letters of the Hindi alphabet. They were thoroughly amused and then we gave them a mango each. Next morning there were five and N.P. suggested that we should give them slates and chalk to write. Within a couple of weeks there were fifteen children, which included three or four girls. They were the younger sisters of the boys, the attraction being the mangoes. The girls were very shy and soft spoken, but they seemed quite keen to learn the alphabet.

Nirmala and I started teaching them in right earnest. I found some of the boys in the age group of eight to ten highly intelligent and their grasp of arithmetic was excellent. I think this was because they were using mental arithmetic in any case. Madame Montessori's method when applied to teaching of Hindi was excellent. Within a couple of months there were about forty children. We were finding it very difficult to manage them. N.P. suggested that we should engage someone to help us, and we were able to find a man who could read and write Hindi and was ready to work with us for a couple of hours on a very reasonable salary, which we could well afford. Nirmala in her own way introduced a little drill and games and taught them the national anthem, while I stressed more on actual teaching of the three Rs. All this lasted for over six months. We were not able to tame the monkeys but were happy that we succeeded with the little ones.

After another few months N.P. was transferred and that meant closing the school. I at least had the satisfaction that within a short period four or five boys were able to fit in class, while the rest went to class two. They all promised to continue their studies in a municipal school which had just opened in our vicinity.

H.K. was not able to find anything suitable and decided to leave Kanpur and ultimately settled in Agra. The Kapurs were well known publishers and printers of Lahore. They were able to come to a settlement with Agra University which gave them a building in the campus where they put up their own machinery and started printing for the University. Nirmala's husband H.K. was put in charge of this unit while his father and younger brother continued with publishing and printing assignments in Delhi. The Agra press did very well and H.K. continued to work there till he passed away in 1971. By that time their elder son Madhu had also joined him. The business was flourishing and as time went by the family decided to move out of the University premises. They bought a piece of land and built a press, Mahim Patran Private Ltd, which today is one of the largest in Agra. Madhu's wife Milan and son Piyush also work there. The ice cream factory is in charge of Arvind, the younger brother. Swami Swayam

Prakash Giri, the youngest brother, took sanyas in 1987. It is remarkable that the Kapurs have retained the tradition of living together as a joint family.

Delhi and Wellington

In January 1952, N.P. was posted to Air Headquarters Delhi as Deputy Director, Technical Services. We were given a flat in Diplomatic Enclave. The rule was that officers with two children were given a flat; officers with three children would get a three bedroom bungalow. In September 1952, Indu was born. We were now allotted a bungalow on Lodhi Road, which was a great boon. After the 1952 general elections, Dewan Sahib was appointed a member of the Election Tribunal to settle any dispute that arose during the elections in Delhi. Rajaji had also given up his job in Patna and came to settle himself in Delhi. So this beautiful bungalow was a godsend for the entire family. I knew that Indu was a very lucky child for us all. In 1953 N.P. was selected to do a Staff College Course in Wellington, which was a very prestigious course, and one could have aspirations of going really high. Fortunately Rajaji got a job in Jaipur, and Dewan Sahib was able to shift to Ambala where he had built a small house. He would come to Delhi wherever the hearing of the cases came up and stay with Prakash Behanji in Todar Mal Road for a few days.

N.P. had a month off before joining the course. So we decided to go by car to Wellington, spending a few days in Agra with Nirmala and also a few days in Pune with K.P. The plan was rather ambitious. We did the first hop to Agra and spent a couple of days with Nirmal, then we stopped at Shivpuri where we had friends. The third stop was Indore where we spent a night in Mhow in the Officers' Mess. The following day we were to spend the night in Nasik, but we reached there by 2 pm and N.P. felt that we could really make it to Pune in about 3 to 4 hours. So we decided to proceed. At about 4 pm or so we were in Igatpuri. I found N.P. trying to use his brakes and they were not working. There was a slight slope and the car went on moving at a fairly high speed, and soon we saw a railway crossing which was closed. On the side there was a car waiting for the gate to open. N.P. saved the car and crashed into the gate, with such force that the gate opened and came back with equal force and banged into our car, leaving the engine in smithereens.

Praveen and Pavan were sitting at the back with the servant. Indu was on my lap in front. I turned around to find all three of them all right. The two gentlemen owners of the car waiting at the crossing rushed to us and opened N.P.'s door and he walked out. They gave N.P. a little brandy, and tea to us. It was a miraculous escape. They put us in their car and drove us to the nearest police station. N.P. then requested the two gentlemen if they could take the family to Bombay which was their destination, to enable him to make arrangements. They readily agreed provided they knew where to drop us. Although we knew quite a few people in Bombay, I could only think of Povaia sisters (Anup Singhji's sisters-in-law) who lived near Chowpatty. I said, *"I will be able to recognize the house but I don't know the address"*.

It was a strange journey, trusting myself and the children to two strangers. One was an Englishman and the other an Indian Muslim both working for an Oil Company. I was very nervous, these sisters were very active, supposing they were out of station, or for that matter had gone out and the house was locked, in that case I would have to go to a hotel, and I had never been in one by myself. I think the two men were a little worried also, supposing she does not recognize the house? However when we reached, they both accompanied us to the house, which was situated a little away from where the car could be parked. We climbed up the little road that led to their house. As

I knocked, promptly the door opened, and the three sisters rushed out and welcomed me with open arms. I thanked the gentleman profusely and they left. Now I was crying, they put me to bed, and went on asking where was N.P. They were very relieved to know that N.P. was alright. They gave me a hot cup of tea and told me to rest while they attended to the children. Within half an hour there was another knock at the door. It was an Air Force doctor. N.P. had telephoned the Bombay Air Force station and requested that a doctor should see the family who may need medical attention. Although he could not give the address, he said that once he got on the steep climb, anybody would be able to tell them where the three sisters lived. The doctor examined us all and congratulated us on our escape. Our beautiful Wolsely took the entire brunt, and we were able to buy only a Morris Minor with the money that the insurance paid us. How much trust we were able to put on strangers is amazing. Today, one would have to think whether it would be safe to travel with strangers!

Life in Wellington, which is near Ooty, was very different. Suddenly N.P. found himself a student, studying, reading, writing and thinking hard to find solutions for tricky problems. I had never seen him reading a novel yet here he was working 10 to 12 hours a day on written material. His determination to do well was over-riding. He did not mind working till late hours writing and rewriting the work that was set until it was to his entire satisfaction.

Praveen and Pavan went to a junior school attached to the Staff College premises. It only catered for children up to the age of 10. As Praveen was one of the oldest children, she felt very responsible for looking after the younger children, and tried to be very helpful to the teachers who were very happy to have such a bright child. For Indu we had an excellent ayah (Rosie) who looked after her very well. Rosie came with us to Kanpur and I found Indu using lots of English words, because that was the language used by Rosie who was from South India.

The other aspect of the Staff College was the social life. Dances and picnics were arranged. Golf, tennis and other games were popular. Bridge formed an important part of the evening programme. Hence N.P. fitted in very well. In the last few months of our stay we started getting letters that Dewan Sahib was not well. He had developed acute arthritis and found moving and walking difficult. It was not possible for N.P. to get leave for the rule was that the officer was given a month's leave before the course and another month after the course; before he went to the next posting.

So when he finished with Wellington, we decided that instead of seeing South India, N.P. would leave for Delhi and I would go to Brother, who was posted in Bombay, till N.P. knew where he was going to be posted. It was fortunate that N.P. was posted to Kanpur, because he was allotted a house immediately and I went to Delhi and brought Dewan Sahib with me to Kanpur.

While in Kanpur I met Mahenderjit's nephew, Captain Saigal, and thought he would be a good match for Tripta (my brother Devji's daughter). It so happened that Bhabji and Tripta were going to Calcutta. I insisted that they broke the journey and stayed with me for a day. I asked Tosh to come over and she met both of them. Soon after I asked her if she liked the girl for their nephew. She was very happy with the idea and wrote to the young man saying that she had seen the girl and liked her very much and if he was interested a photo could be sent. He wrote back to say that he would like to meet the girl. Her answer was that they are a very respectable family and you can meet her only if you are going to say yes. His reply was, in that case I trust your judgment and said yes without meeting her. My family also had enough confidence in me. The fact that he belonged to a very respectable family and was an Army Officer was enough. So the wedding was arranged for 30 April 1955 in Calcutta. With time, thinking can also change. Father now wanted the Barat to be put up in a hotel. It meant saving so much botheration, only a little extra money and everybody was happy. The Barat consisted of about 15 people. Light refreshments were served to all the guests at the wedding but dinner in the house was served to about 40 guests (they had about 25 local guests) and the family. Would I have the courage to arrange a marriage like that today? Certainly not!

In the meanwhile, Father had undergone a cataract operation and was confined to bed without any movement. He developed static pneumonia but he insisted that the wedding was not to be postponed. The last time he got out of his bed and wore his turban was for the *Milni* [44] with the bridegroom's father on the wedding day. The wedding went off smoothly and after the *Doli* [45] the following day, he found breathing difficult, and was put in an oxygen tent. He lived for 20 days, and passed away peacefully on 20 May 1955. What a good life, peaceful in life and death.

He left a very clear will and a very moderate legacy. The house in which he lived went to the four sons, with some cash to be divided among all his children. The house could conveniently be divided into three portions, so my eldest brother got some cash for not sharing the house. Fortunately he bought a farm in Chattarpur near Delhi, and the price of both the Calcutta property as well as the Delhi property rose by leaps and bounds. The sisters also utilized the money well. Sarlabibi bought some land in Sundernagar, Delhi. I used my share in building a house in Defence Colony and Nirmala set up a small ice-cream factory, which were all very good investments. He said no further charity was necessary as he had given away what he wanted during his life time.

Back to Delhi and We Build a House

A few years after Partition, the Government set up a scheme such that all officers of the Armed Forces who had property in the Punjab would be allotted small plots of land of about 300 square yards, at very nominal rates, to enable them to build houses for themselves. The land was called Cloakery out in the wilderness. Both N.P. and K.P. were quite reluctant to accept the land, they felt that the plots were too small and the scheme would not take off. Dewan Sahib did not listen to them and just paid the money on his sons' behalf saying, *"The Government is after all giving you something, why should you refuse it"*. That is how we acquired the land!

In 1956, N.P. was posted back in Delhi and I went to Ambala to Dewan Sahib waiting for N.P. to be allotted accommodation. Dewan Sahib knew his son well and realized that whatever money my Father had left would just be blown away in holidays and the like, and he encouraged N.P. to build a house on the land that was allotted to us. This money was certainly not enough but Dewan Sahib encouraged him and promised to give him Rs 20,000 as part of his inheritance. N.P. thus got busy with the plans and two young architects who were quite new to the profession worked very hard and we built a lovely two bedroom house with a drawing room, dining room, a kitchen, and a servants quarter with an independent staircase, in case we wanted to have further additions. Ours was the third house in Defence Colony and lots of officers who saw the house were so impressed that Bawa Bhatia, who were our architects, became very popular and were able to build several houses in that area. We had to take a further loan, which was paid off slowly with the rent that we got. We were able to get a tenant even before the house was fully ready.

I had a five months' wait in Ambala before N.P. got a flat. While in Ambala I engaged a tutor for Praveen and Pavan for Hindi and Maths. Their standard of English was good. When I got to Delhi, I tried to put Praveen in the Convent school, but they refused, as there was no seat vacant. The defence personnel had been facing this problem of educating their children. With frequent transfers, the children were affected adversely and would sometime lose a year through no fault of their own. The Government had just started the Air Force Central School for older children and the Bal Bharti as a junior school. So we just put Praveen in the Central School which was very close to our house in Teen Murti Lane, and Pavan also joined her after a few months. It was a co-educational school open to all children of defence forces. Their extra circular activities were fine, but that concentrated stress on studies alone was missing. The children enjoyed going to school and got satisfactory reports. Indu went to the Carmel Convent. This time we had a long spell in Delhi. The Gymkhana Club was close-by and the children used the Club mostly for swimming and Sunday outings. There was a library also but the children's section was not so well equipped. I encouraged them to take part in all the Club activities like attending the Diwali and Christmas parties when the children were expected to come in fancy dress. I would want them to think carefully, so that their dresses would be effective and yet not too expensive. Their friends were always made welcome and I never objected if they visited their friends provided they were within walking or cycling distance.

During our stay in Delhi, N.P. got an opportunity of going to Dehra Dun for the RIMC Old Boys reunion.

I accompanied him and it was a pleasure to meet so many officers from his school, and their wives; and thoroughly enjoyed our stay of about two days there. For N.P. it was a great joy to meet so many of his school friends who were now senior officers in the Army. N.P. was the only one who was in the Air Force. Fortunately for him, he had such quick promotion in the Air Force that he was more or less at par with his class mates. The RIMC, which was originally called the Royal Indian Military College, became after Independence the Rashtriya (national) Indian Military College, so the abbreviation has not changed.

At one Old Boys' reunion, N.P. spoke to Air Marshal Mookerjee and suggested that he should take a helicopter to Dehra Dun and land in the large compound of the college. It was difficult to find suitable young men for the Air Force because people thought that the Air Force meant greater risk. N.P thought it important to attract young minds to join. Air Marshal Mookerjee readily agreed. When N.P. landed, most of the children became very excited and rushed to receive him. It so happened that General Thimaya, Chief of Army Staff, entered the college by car at the same time, and there were very few students to receive him. The sporting spirit was so great that the General shook hands with N.P. saying *"You have stolen the show!"*

There was much laughter and merriment and a great sense of camaraderie.

We had very close contact with General Virendra Singh (also from RIMC) and his wife Mohini, whom we met in Madras soon after our marriage. The men were friends, but both Mohini and I liked each other very much and over the years our friendship became very sincere and caring. It so happened that N.P. and Virendra were posted in Delhi at the same time. We got together almost every Sunday, had lunch, and played bridge. When we left Delhi we still kept in touch, as we went to Kasauli very often from Delhi, Patiala and Chandigarh. They had their own house in Kasauli, and very often we were there at the same time. Many times if we went for just a weekend we would stay with them, otherwise we stayed in the Kasauli Club which had very comfortable rooms. There were other friends like General Prem Bhagat (the first Indian officer to win the Victoria Cross in the Second World War) whom we met quite often. General Bhagat came to Wellington as the first Indian Commander of the Staff College, when N.P. had just finished his course. Unfortunately, Prem Bhagat died soon after he retired and N.P., as the most senior officer present for the Old Boys reunion, read his obituary with tearful eyes.

K.P. gave us a lovely Cocker Spaniel in 1956. The children were absolutely thrilled to have this lovely animal and she was the pet of the entire household. For some reason K.P. took her back after six months and Pavan was extremely disappointed. He was determined to buy a dog immediately. We then bought an Alsatian pup, Rex, which was with us for a number of years. We were in Delhi in a big house with a large garden and the dog was playful and obedient. I did find the early period of training a bit difficult. The feeding and his care were left to me, and very soon I was able to look after him. I think the dog was very much attached to Pavan, who spent a lot of time playing with him in the garden. He lived till 1962, when he had to be put to sleep after he developed some serious disease and was hospitalized. Soon after, we were presented with a Russian Samoyed by Mrs Kamla Saigal. Indu was about 10 years old and was able to hold the pup in her two hands, but within six months he had grown so much that many times when playing Indu would fall down, but gradually Kazbeck became very gentle and obedient. By 1964, both Praveen and Pavan had left home, and so Kazbeck became essentially Indu's dog and she gave him a lot of care.

I was strolling in the garden one evening when a lady with a little child walked in. I did not know her. She came up to me and introduced herself. *"I am Pushpa Hidayatullah and this is my daughter"*. I thought I had heard wrong. I knew that Justice Hidayatullah, a judge of the Supreme Court, lived on Race Course Road and we were in Teen Murti Lane, but it was the next house to ours. When she said Pushpa I was a bit confused. She repeated herself and said *"I am a Hindu Gujarati married to Justice Hidayatullah"*. I naturally asked her to come in and she came straight to the point and said *"My daughter is called Avni. She has a heart condition and we are not sending her to school. I understand that you have a daughter almost her age. I would like them to be friends"*. My response was spontaneous *"Certainly"*, and I called Indu and said *"Indu, here is a new friend for you, Avni, she lives next door and you can play together"*. Mrs Hidayatullah spoke very sweetly to Indu, and said *"You can come over when ever you like"*. After a couple of days I asked Pavan to take Indu to their house. He agreed, but reluctantly, and came home after a while. He said *"Mummy, Avni has got a brother my age so we have also become friends"*. One day while Avni and Indu were playing in the garden, I found them running a race. Indu was naturally ahead, but I was very frightened to see Avni panting and breathing with a lot of difficulty. I was panic stricken. I just took her in my arms and rushed to their house. Mrs Hidayatullah was very understanding and explained to Indu *"She cannot run, but you can play other games with her"*. I was very nervous and made it clear to her that sending Indu to their house was no problem, but I felt a sense of responsibility when Avni came to us. She was delighted with the proposal and after that generally Indu and Pavan went to their house, and also went out for long drives and outings with them. After work, the only interest that the parents had was their children and it gave them great pleasure to include Pavan and Indu in the outings they gave their children. After a couple of years, we were going to Kashmir for a holiday, and the Hidayatullahs were going to England for heart surgery for Avni. The little child died in the operation theatre and when we returned from Kashmir we naturally called on them. I had to explain to Indu that Avni had died and she refused to go to their house. Pushpaji requested me to send Indu to see her and I persuaded her to go at least once to see Aunty. Next day Mrs Hidayatullah came to see me and with tears in her eyes she said *"You have got an exceptional child, I asked her what would you like out of Avni's things. A dress or a toy or anything you want. She first kept quiet and then said, I would like to have a picture of Avni"*. And she gave me a photograph which Indu still has. Pavan and Arshad continued to be friends. Justice Hidayatullah became the Chief Justice and then the Vice-President of India, but we were posted to Kanpur and did not have much occasion to meet. I recently met Arshad after more than forty years and had the same feeling of affection for him which I had when he was a child.

As the children were growing up, we knew that we could not afford to send them to Public Schools. At the same time we wanted to do our best and chose the best local schools. During the summer holidays we would always make a plan and go to some hill station. From Kanpur, we went to Nainital, and from Delhi we made two trips to Kashmir and several trips to Kasauli. We generally booked Army accommodation at a nominal rent. These were designated as holiday homes, small comfortable, two bedroom flats or barracks, for officers of the Armed Forces.

N.P. was keen that all three children should learn swimming. Pavan was given a golf set when he was twelve years old, and was able to practise and learn in Gulmarg. He also became interested in sailing.

Pavan left for the National Defence Academy (NDA) when he was just about 15 years old. Whenever he came home for holidays, N.P. wanted him to learn driving. From 1964, Indu was the only one with us. Her schooling from 1966 was in Patiala in the Yadavindra Public School (YPS).

In 1957, we were still in Delhi when Republic Day was to be celebrated on 26 January. Hectic activity ensued. On either side of Raj Path seating accommodation was being arranged. Elaborate arrangements for car parking and passes were issued for seating in reserved enclosures. Our seats were in the Defence enclosure and we were expected to be in our seats by 7 am. N.P. had been busy for nearly a month and had visited Agra, Ambala, Halwara, and Jullunder. I knew that he was a little excited and nervous, but I pretended that I did not notice anything. On the night of 25 January we put on the alarm for 5.30 am. I had to have my tea, get the children ready and give them an early breakfast. January is bitterly cold in Delhi so after putting pullovers, coats, caps and mittens, I carried a blanket, and a picnic basket full of food. We reached Raj Path at exactly 7 am. It was interesting to watch people rushing to the enclosures which their passes indicated (we were in the Defence enclosure) and trying to get seats from where they would be able to get the best view. At 9 am, Dr Rajendra Prasad, our first President, drove in an open carriage pulled by several horses. The Army bands followed with the Cavalry and Infantry regiments in their colourful uniforms, the pomp and splendour was a sight worth seeing. After the Army, which was the main wing of the Armed Forces, came the Navy and the Air Force.

The bands and the marching of the Air Force was never of a very high order, and being the youngest wing they did not have very much to show on the ground. When I saw this I felt a little sense of disappointment. Was N.P. working and worrying so hard for this? Then suddenly there was a great hue and cry and clapping, the fly-past was in progress, leaving behind orange, white and green lines on the horizon, and thousands of balloons of the three colours filled the sky. The fly-past certainly stole the show and I could see relief and happiness in N.P.'s face. Everything had gone off very well. It is very difficult for the public to realize how much work goes into an exhibition of this sort. Different kinds of aircraft stationed in different places have to be punctual to a second if they have to fly in formation: any delay can prove to be fatal. It involves a lot of practice and precision. Now when I see young people showing boredom and lack of interest, I am sad that they think watching these parades even on TV is a waste of time.

Being a senior officer in Air Headquarters involves certain other duties besides the office work. In 1959 General Eisenhower was visiting India. N.P. and I were expected to be at the airport along with others to receive him. We got ready a couple of hours before he was due to land and were on our way to the airport which was about 6 or 7 km away from our house. I personally thought it was too early but N.P. who was very particular about punctuality preferred to leave early. We had hardly done about a couple of kilometres, and were on the Kitchener Road now called Sardar Patel Marg, when Pandit Nehru's car passed us, and then within two minutes, I don't know exactly what happened, but there was a terrific traffic jam with hundreds of cars in front of us and hundreds behind. There was a four deep line of cars but with no movement. We just stayed put in one place for over an hour – there seemed to be no movement. I did not feel nervous for all the cars were stationary with people with Gandhi caps who may have been Ministers, and people in uniforms with shining buttons and medals on their chests just sitting and twiddling their thumbs. A movement started once General Eisenhower had landed and taken a detour through empty streets and the traffic was allowed to move when the traffic police wanted the space where we were stranded for his procession to pass. Once the movement started it got worse, for everyone wanted to move at the same time. We got home after a four hours outing and not even a glimpse of the President who was brought to his destination, Rashtra Pati Bhavan. He only waved to the crowd that was waiting around the Raj Path and Vijay Chowk. However, when Queen Elizabeth came the following year there was no traffic jam and her reception at the airport passed off smoothly. I chose not to venture but N.P. was on duty and came home quite happy. The traffic police had learned how to control the cars. The ones that did not have the right poster sticker were just not allowed to be on the route and were turned away while several kilometres away from the airport. In the evening we attended a big reception at the Rashtra Pati Bhavan.

In November 1960 N.P. rang me up from the office in a broken voice saying *"Something terrible has happened"*. *"Kya Hua what has happened?"* *"Air Marshal"*, he said and could not continue. *"What has happened to the Air Marshal?"* *"He is dead"*, and he put down the phone. I knew that a goodwill mission led by Air Marshal Mookerjee, the Chief of the Air Staff, had gone to Japan. I naturally presumed that it must have been an air crash and I rang back to N.P. and said *"What about all the others?"* He answered *"The rest are alright. We are awaiting details but it appears that it happened when he was attending the last farewell dinner"*. My next thought was that it must have been a heart attack. But I was wrong. The postmortem revealed that a fish bone got stuck in his throat and he went to the toilet. He was followed by the aide-de-camp (ADC) who was waiting outside. When he did not come out after ten minutes, the ADC knocked at the door and there was no response, he reported the matter, the door was opened and the Air Marshal was lying dead. Mrs Mookerjee, who was by herself in Delhi with a young son, showed great forbearance and dignity. The whole country was in shock. His body was brought back after two days and a very befitting funeral was accorded to him with full military honours. The whole of Delhi was lined up on either side of the route from Akbar Road to Nigambodh Ghat. Everybody felt a sense of great loss. He had proved to be a man of great vision with no airs about him. He had all the qualities of a soldier and leadership and yet put simple human values of kindness and sympathy on a high pedestal. Air Marshal Engineer, who was at that moment shaping the Hindustan Aeronautics Ltd in Bangalore, was recalled and made the Air Chief.

Dewan Sahib had developed arthritis in 1954, was now getting worse day by day and we insisted that he shifted to us, as we had a beautiful bungalow. He held on to the Election Tribunal till the end and was able to give the verdict. This spell of about 3 years gave him a lot of mental and financial stability. His condition went on deteriorating. There were his three old servants attending to him day and night as he needed full attention all the time. A doctor was engaged to come and see him at least twice a week for a general check up. He was extremely fussy about cleanliness in spite of being so ill. He never refused a sponge or a daily change of bed linen. He was quite exacting but was very fond of us and blessed us for looking after him so well. Raja Bhai and Chandji used to come to see him quite often. K.P. and his family were in Simla and visited from time to time.

In the summer of 1960 we had gone to Kashmir for a holiday. Raja Bhai Sahib and Chandji shifted to our house to be with Dewan Sahib. After about three weeks we received a telegram from Rajaji that Father was seriously ill. We were in Gulmarg. We rang up our friend Balwant Kapur to make arrangements for our return. We would spend a night with them in Srinagar where we reached in the evening. N.P. and I were feeling rather anxious and after dinner Balwant insisted that we go out for a cup of coffee. I was too tired and wanted to rest with the children, but N.P. went out. When he returned, I asked him the time. He looked at his wrist to find the watch was missing. He rushed downstairs to the car and looked high and low but could not find it. He came up rather disappointed and I said *"We must tell Balwant that the watch is lost"*, but N.P. said *" It is lost, it is no use telling him, he has done so much for us already, why bother him. In any case I don't mind losing it, if I can see my father alive and better"*.

I retorted *"This has nothing to do with your father, it was a gold watch which you will never be able to replace. Where is the harm in telling the host, it will only mean a trip to the coffee shop. Had it been a fountain pen, I would say forget about it"*. We went to bed. Early next morning N.P. went down once again and looked for the watch and found it. He came up very happy. We left for Jammu by a station wagon and on reaching there, the luggage was shifted into a railway compartment. I opened my bag to check the list of the packages we had. Much to my amazement I saw that the fountain pen from my bag was missing. I just kept quiet. On reaching home we found Father much better. The incident brooks no explanation.

Dewan Sahib passed away in November 1960 after a long illness. He left a clear will which said that everything that he possessed was to be shared by the three sons. But they thought a little differently, and some cash was given to the sisters also.

The three servants who had served him very faithfully were also rewarded, but we did not need them anymore. At the same time, we had no desire to terminate their services. Fortunately one of them was keen to get back to his village, the cook was taken over by Minnie, K.P.'s eldest daughter, and we were left with one, Sheru, who used to clean the floors and looked after the cow in Ferozepore. We promoted him to the rank of a bearer and I must say that in spite of all the silly mistakes he made, N.P. always laughed, instead of being angry or upset. So we acquired a faithful servant who stayed with us for several years, till K.P. wanted him to go to the farm which he had acquired in Rampur.

During Dewan Sahib's illness, my mind also required some stimulus. Seeing so much pain in the house, I was now looking for some spiritual peace. Sarlabibi was in Delhi and used to attend a Mangal Satsang on Prithvi Raj Road. There was a lady Sanyasi called Mata Brahm Jyoti who conducted a kirtan at the residence of Mrs K G Khosla. I started going to this Satsang regularly and found that besides prayers and Bhajans, the discourse that the lady gave was more in the form of a class where she took up a religious book and explained every verse in detail. She was now teaching Patanjali's Yoga Darshan [46]. She insisted that we learn each *sutra* [47] that she taught, by heart. She was slow but very thorough, and I was able to understand Patanjali's approach of self-realization, the discipline that is required and the qualities that have to be developed to enable a person to see his own real image: that is the God within, which resides in all beings, by meditation. And the first step to enable a person to even think of meditation is doing yogic exercise, which only makes a person physically fit, for ill health is the first obstacle that has to be removed.

The teachings of the Gita were also included. In short I must admit that though the fundamentals of good clean living, and the benefits of honesty, kindness and truthfulness were inculcated in my childhood, I benefited a lot from Mataji's discourses.

During our stay in Delhi, there were quite a few weddings in the family, and both N.P. and I were very active participants in making all the necessary arrangements. Saroj, Sarupji's daughter, was married to Bir Thakker in Delhi in 1957, and all the arrangements were left to Nirmala and myself. Soon after, Krishna, Devji's second daughter, got married to G.P. Khungar. In 1961 Arjun, our eldest nephew, married Amrita Soni. Brother was posted in Bombay and arrived on the day of the wedding. Our house was the centre for all the guests till on the wedding eve we were accommodated by the Sonis as a Barat.

In the meanwhile, Kusum got married in London to Kartar Malhotra and I had to arrange and send her wedding sari, which got to her a day before the marriage, through the pilot who was flying Pandit Nehru to London. Kusum and Kartar returned to

India soon after their marriage and Kartar got a job with Burmah Shell. Their son was born in Delhi the following year, and I was there in hospital to welcome my sister's first born grandson and the first great-grandson of my parents, Ashwan.

Nirmala and I were able to arrange another wedding at very short notice and that was Rupa, Devji's youngest daughter, who married Teg Bahadur Kaushal. This marriage took place in our house in Teen Murti Lane.

Another marriage, which must be mentioned, was Sheila's, daughter of Prakash Behanji. It was a love marriage and inter-caste. Raju was from Rajasthan and his father was keen that we held the marriage in Ajmer where he was posted, according to their own style and custom. We agreed to have the wedding there, provided they made all the arrangements as we knew nothing about Ajmer. This suited them. It was one of the most enjoyable weddings, as we were saved all the botheration of attending to the Barat. In fact they received our family, put cars at our disposal, and made all the arrangements for our stay. We were about 15 people: the Varma Brothers, Raja Bhai, myself, and three or four friends of Sheila. After the wedding, Jijaji wanted to clear the bill. They were very considerate and said just leave a sum he thought appropriate, and they accepted the amount very graciously.

Kanpur Again

Indu was still in school, when N.P. was posted to Kanpur once again in January 1964 as an Air Commodore commanding the Base Repair Depot (BRD). We were very happy. We left Praveen with Sarlabibi to do her final year in College. Pavan went to the National Defence Academy (NDA) near Pune and only Indu was now with us.

Air Marshal Harjinder Singh had retired and N.P. was the senior-most technical officer in the Air Force. A new command called the Maintenance Command had been established, which was headed by an Air Vice-Marshal from the general branch (pilots) in Nagpur.

Air Vice-Marshal Harjinder Singh, from whom N.P. was now going to take charge, was the senior most officer of the technical branch. He was a man with great vision and made a very successful officer. He was responsible for the manufacturing of the Avro aircraft. He also held a flying license and used to fly privately. His wife Beant was equally outstanding. She had no formal education and came from a well-to-do family from a Punjab village. She took very little time to get into the ways of service life and proved to be a very good hostess. She was fond of animals, always kept a dog, and small poultry and a cow in the house. She learned to drive a car, and later on learned to fly also, and held a proper license. It has been a life-long friendship with her, and Satto, her younger sister, who lived with them.

In Delhi, we were family-oriented, there was hardly any interaction with the Air Force officers. The concentration was on the Club and our relations. In Kanpur there was a lot of interaction with the officers, and we had a very busy social life with the civilians and with the European community as well.

In 1964, when we were in Kanpur, we had a cow which was presented to us by Air Marshal Harjinder Singh, who was retiring, and N.P. had taken over the command from him. Our old servant Sheru was very good with animals as he used to take care of the buffalo and a cow that Dewan Sahib had in Ferozepore.

After a few months of our stay in Kanpur I developed a small cyst in my breast. I went to the doctor who assured me that it was nothing serious but it had to be removed. I think I saw him on a Monday and he told me to come on a Friday which was his operation day. I was naturally quite worried. On Monday evening Sheru came to me and said *"The cow is quite unwell, she has not eaten anything for a whole day"*. I told him that it was too late in the evening to send for a vet, but we would attend to her the next morning. I was feeling quite worried and upset over my own problem and was tossing and turning in bed the whole night. At last when I dozed off I felt someone saying to me *"Why are you feeling so worried, Cow is a Mother, she has taken over all your troubles"*. And I woke up with a start and found Sheru saying *"The cow is going"*. *"Where?"* I said. *"She is dying"*, he answered. I rushed out and saw the cow. She was very uncomfortable and could not breathe properly. I rushed in and rang up N.P. who had already gone to the office and told him to ring for a doctor and come home immediately. He sensed the anxiety in my voice, and both he and the doctor arrived within fifteen minutes. The verdict of the doctor was quite clear. There was no chance of her survival and he could send a vehicle to carry the animal to the hospital to save us the pain of the animal's death in the house. I said I would ring him up if we needed the transport and he left.

By this time lots of people mostly from the servants' quarters gathered and started advising. Some said give her gur [48] and Ajevain [49]. One of them said that he knew a man who was very good with animals. *"Shall I fetch him, he does not live very far"*, I said *"Yes"*, and within a few minutes the man arrived. He did not take even a minute to say that the only chance of her survival was an operation. He said to me *"Mataji, the cow is going, I have to use the knife if I try to save her. I am a Muslim. I should not be blamed if she does not live"*. I assured him and thanked him even for trying. He just put his knife across part of the neck which was swollen and buckets of puss came out. Within ten minutes she was breathing much more comfortably. I stood by her the whole day and found that she was definitely better. This man came to see the cow every day for a week, and then at intervals of four or five days. It took her two months to get well. On Friday the doctor removed my cyst under local anesthesia and I came home ready for a game of bridge in the evening. Would I have given the care I gave the cow, if I did not have that vision? I wonder!

Another Difficult Chapter of My Life

The maintenance command was in the charge of Air Vice-Marshal O.P. Mehra, who had been a friend of ours for years. In fact we had lived in the same house for several months in Ambala in 1947, and were instrumental in arranging his brother's marriage to the daughter of a very good friend. N.P. found it little irritating to take orders from a pilot who knew little of the technicalities and the actual needs of the department. Although they had been friends all along, suddenly things seemed to change and there were actual differences. N.P. sought an interview with the Chief which was refused. N.P. felt most hurt and insulted and one day said to me *"I feel like resigning"*. I just turned around and said, *"Don't be silly, why should you resign? Differences will always occur. That does not mean anything. Nobody can remove you from your chair. We have to think about our children now"*. But he had already put in his papers. Within a fortnight his resignation was accepted, something unheard of, for normally it took months before an officer could be released. He was given two months' leave that he was entitled to before retirement. This was August 1965. The fact that he had resigned, and its acceptance, came to me together. I was shocked and completely bewildered. The same evening I rang up Tosh to say that we were coming over to meet them. The news came as a great surprise to them also, but they took up a good stand and did not blame N.P. They had a big house and an annex of three rooms with an independent kitchen and two bathrooms, which they were planning to rent out. They insisted that we move into this annex. I thanked them and said that we shall think about it, but N.P. was adamant to cut off all connections with the Air Force and shifted into this flat within a week or so.

Group Captain Raj K.S. Marya, who was second in command, was a very good friend of ours and lived in the bungalow next door. I had known his wife Prem much before she married. Their daughter Uma was Indu's age, and they both enjoyed going to school together, as well as swimming at the Club which was a walking distance from our house. Raj Marya arranged a lovely farewell party for us and asked for a list of friends that we would like to invite. Our list was fairly long. Everybody made it a point to attend. The arrangements were perfect, but the spirit of joy was lacking. Raj Marya gave a touching speech and presented us with a silver tea set on behalf of the officers of the station. Besides him, all his other colleagues in Delhi, particularly Air Commodore G. B. Singh, Group Captain A.S. Rikhey, and Group Captain K.N. Chawla were feeling very hurt and upset also. K.N. Chawla later retired as Air Commodore while the other three went on to become Air Vice-Marshals.

While N.P. was still on leave, the 1965 war with Pakistan started. The technical officers were feeling very bad about N.P. and requested the Chief to recall him because of the emergency. He told them that if N.P. of his own accord wanted to withdraw the resignation in view of the war he would reconsider. N.P. was now not in a mood to return. It is interesting to note that the officer who took over from N.P. was decorated for exceptional service that he rendered to BRD (he had been there hardly a month). Soon after, a technical officer took over the Maintenance Command. So I now have the satisfaction that his sacrifice for the technical branch was not wasted, but I felt very differently then for it meant a complete upheaval in our life.

After the initial shock, I found myself very upset and angry with N.P. for not having consulted me before taking such a drastic step. What kind of a successful marriage was this? After 24 years together he did not feel the necessity of ascertaining my feelings. But I never got an opportunity of showing my displeasure. N.P. promptly got into a depression and it broke my heart to see the misery on his face. Our friends continued to behave as if nothing had happened and went on inviting us. I would always accept the invitations for I feared that if we stopped meeting friends he might become a recluse. Finding a suitable job seemed very difficult. Having been such a senior officer in the Air Force, he certainly would not fit in a flying club from where he started his career. He had no idea of the commercial world, and had no business acumen. Where could he fit in? After working for the Government, company jobs seemed impossible for a man who knew nothing about the private sector.

Before our posting to Kanpur as Air Officer Commanding (AOC), N.P. had been offered the General Managership of Hindustan Aeronautics Ltd. (HAL), but he preferred to remain in the Air Force. Air Vice-Marshal Ranjan Dutt then became the Managing Director. I now suggested to N.P. that he should write to Ranjan Dutt and ask him if he could be fitted in as the number 2. *"Let your ego not get in the way, it will be a prestigious job and with your seniority you cannot accept just any job that may come your way, after all Ranjan is a good friend and you can write a private letter to him"*. N.P. now did not have the courage to refuse me and wrote a Demi-Official (DO) Letter. Ranjan promptly wrote back a very encouraging letter and this changed N.P.'s mood a little. My Brother asked him to go to Calcutta and he would introduce him to some big firms. N.P. went but it only proved to be a good holiday. In December, my nephew Rajen, Sarlabibi's son, was getting married and we decided to go to Delhi. From there we went to Chandigarh to meet Air Vice-Marshal Harjinder Singh who was now aviation adviser to the Punjab Government. He promised N.P. that he would be able to find him a suitable position within a month or two. Meanwhile we got a message from Air Vice-Marshal Mehra that he had arranged an interview with a firm in Bombay in which N.P. could fit in, and he should proceed to Bombay immediately. I was highly appreciative of this gesture and persuaded N.P. to go to Bombay. He came back quite satisfied with the terms that were offered. They had also promised him a small flat in Juhu. They said that they would draw up a proper contract and he could join in April. Soon after one fine morning we got a telegram from Air Vice-Marshal Harjinder Singh that the Punjab Government was ready to take him as their Chief Technical Officer and he would be posted in Patiala. After a gap of about eight months we now had two offers to choose from. I give full credit to Mahenderjit Singh for insisting that the Government job in Patiala was the right choice. Knowing N.P.'s temperament and club-going habit, he made N.P. realize that he would be at a loose end every evening. The entry fee to a prestigious club was prohibitive; besides the waiting list was always very long. After living in luxurious bungalows, a small flat in Bombay would be claustrophobic. Besides these private firms may just give a month's notice, and the security that he would have in a government job could never be available in a private firm. So once again we decided to join the government.

Besides helping us to make this decision, I must say how grateful we were to Mahendra and Tosh for extending us their support in our hour of adversity. We stayed in their flat for eight months and they refused to take any rent. As there was no separate electricity connection, they also paid the electricity bills. We used their telephones and there was never an occasion that if somebody rang up for us, we would not get the message immediately. In short, they made us so welcome and comfortable, that I always look back on that period with a great sense of gratitude to them. They really proved that a friend in need is a valued friend indeed. Their moral support and advice of going to Patiala was of great value. We never regretted our choice.

The work in Patiala was interesting but not as stressful as that in the Air Force. We were allotted a large 4-bedroom house with an acre of land. We joined the Baradari Club immediately, and fitted very well into Patiala life. Praveen was now in her final year of her Master of Arts degree, and we left her in Agra with Nirmala for doing her final year from Agra University. We tried to put Indu in the best local school, but found that she was rather uncomfortable after being in a convent. The Principal of the Yadavindra Public School (YPS) was a European, a member of the Club and N.P. mentioned the problem to him. He straightaway offered to take her in his school which was basically meant for boys. He said that there were about a dozen girls who were from the south, who knew no Punjabi, and he had accommodated them. Indu was keen to change her school and she went to the YPS very happily. There was one other girl in her class, so the two of them became very good friends. Shashi and Shobha Kulkarni were the daughters of the Income Tax Commissioner and both the sisters used to come to our house and Indu spent quite a few evenings with them when N.P. and I went to the Club. Life once again was normal.

The Nehru-Shastri Era 1947-1966

Immediately after Partition, India had to face the gigantic problem of refugees. While this problem was being sorted out, another major problem arose. The Pakistan army was intruding into Kashmir and the Maharajah of Kashmir acceded to India. The Indian Army went into action and was able to throw back the intruders and would have pushed them out completely, but Pandit Nehru chose to take the problem to the United Nations. A cease fire was ordered and a line of control was drawn on the basis of where the two armies stood. This line was like the Berlin wall, families were separated and there was discontent on both sides. Pandit Nehru was an idealist and a democrat at heart and wanted to abide by the decision of the UN, which itself was a new organization. A plebiscite was suggested and Pandit Nehru agreed to let the people decide which country they wanted to join. This meant that Pakistan would first have to vacate the land they had occupied. They never vacated the area, the plebiscite never took place, and the problem today is still unresolved.

As a simple housewife I failed to understand why the intruders had not been thrown out completely. The Maharajah had acceded to India, a right that was granted to all the native states. People worshipped Nehru and thought that he could do no wrong and accepted the situation. It was an open secret that Sardar Patel and Nehru had differences. While the former was in charge of Home Affairs, the latter had the portfolio of Foreign Affairs. Had the portfolios been the other way around, would the Kashmir issue have taken the shape it did? I wonder. Anyway, Kashmir has taken a big toll of human lives and material resources of both countries, and to this day has eluded a solution.

In 1950 the Indian Constitution was drawn up, drafted mainly by Dr Ambedkar, an eminent lawyer of immense knowledge, belonging to the scheduled caste, and Sir Maurice Gwyer, the Chief Justice of India, who supervised and assisted him. Bharat India was declared a Federal Republic. In 1952 the first general elections were held. We were excited like little children who were going to participate in a big show. Congress was the only party that had done maximum work to gain independence. The Muslim League after Partition had lost its strength, there was the Communist Party which had some influence in Bengal but was far from being a nationalist party. When a person of Pandit Nehru's stature was at the helm of affairs, who wanted to vote for anybody else? With no hesitation, the country returned the Congress Party to power in 1952, 1957, and 1962.

Under Nehru started the first Five Year Plan which stressed irrigation to make the country self-sufficient in food. The Bhakra Nangal Dam and Damodar Valley Dams helped agriculture and the Green Revolution. The second Five Year Plan focused on steel and industrialisation. A Commission worked on the re-organization of States on linguistic lines. In short, India seemed to be on the road to progress.

In 1962 when we were in Delhi, India suffered a big shock when China invaded India on the Tibetan border. The Dalai Lama had left Tibet in 1960 and sought asylum in India and was living in Dharamsala. We had been hearing the slogan *"Hindi Chini Bhai Bhai"*, meaning that the Indians and Chinese were like brothers. It was distressing to hear Pandit Nehru addressing the nation on the radio in a broken voice to tell us, *"Whom we considered a friend has stabbed us in the back"*, or words to that effect. India was not prepared for war in the cold mountainous region of the Tibetan border. Soldiers became ill, and even before they faced the enemy they were stricken with frostbite, losing their toes and fingers. Hectic activity started in Delhi. N.P. also flew to Chushul, the highest airfield in the world to see what kind of foreign aircraft could land there. However the Chinese withdrew of their own accord within a few days, having established their supremacy. It was undoubtedly an unfought war. Pandit Nehru was a broken man, but he continued to be the Prime Minister until he died in May 1964. The whole of India, indeed the whole world, mourned his loss. He will go down in history as a great patriot and a true democrat.

In November 1963, six officers were killed in a helicopter crash. Their remains were brought to Delhi. Those dead included Air Vice-Marshal Pinto, General Daulat Singh, a Brigadier and two other officers of the Air Force. Air Vice-Marshal Pinto was a personal friend of ours. His young daughter Valerie and Indu were in the same class at Carmel Convent. N.P. would drop them to school and Mrs Pinto used to bring them back. Mrs Daulat Singh and I used to play a lot of bridge together. Besides being a great loss to the Services, it was a personal loss to us. This had a great impact on Indu, because she had already lost a friend in Avni, and now Valerie had lost her father. Three funerals were arranged: a Hindu, Christian and a Parsi, at different times to enable people to attend them, and pay their last respects to the departed souls with full military honours. The very next day the world mourned the loss of J.F. Kennedy. I thought that the days of political assassination were over. After Abraham Lincoln, this was another political murder and the world lost another great democrat. I never realized that a period of political assassinations was coming to India also.

After Nehru who, was the big question? When Pandit Nehru died, the choice fell on the unassuming Lal Bahadur Shastri who had dedicated his life to the cause of Independence and worked shoulder to shoulder with Nehru and Patel. He also proved to be a man of great courage and grit. At this time there was a lot of discontent in the southern states because people in the north wanted to do away with English and establish Hindi as the national language. It was extremely difficult for the southern states to learn Hindi and then compete for the Services. Shastriji had the foresight to retain both Hindi and English as official languages. English is a world language and it has proved to be a great boon to India which has been able to progress in the field of science and technology. Today we find Indians working all over the world because of the advantage of the knowledge that English gives us. Shastri was ready to take on Pakistan in 1965 when it first tried to enter the Rann of Kutch and later intrude into Kashmir. The Indian Army entered Pakistan and within three weeks Pakistan was seeking a truce. A treaty was drawn up in Tashkent, and it was decided that the Kashmir issue would be sorted out by dialogue. It was a great victory for India but unfortunately Shastri died of a massive heart attack the same night. He had been Prime Minister for hardly a year and a half but within that short period he achieved a lot and his slogan for India's progress was *Jai Jawan, Jai Kisan* – Victory for the soldier, and the agriculturalist.

Shastri had inducted Indira Gandhi as a Minister in his cabinet, in charge of Information and Broadcasting. The choice for Prime Ministership now fell upon her. We were all very happy to have a woman Prime Minister. It showed the world how progressive we were. She was the only daughter of Pandit Nehru and was a most uncontroversial figure. In all probability the men in the cabinet must have thought that a woman who had never held any office would play into their hands. But the future unveiled a very different picture.

Praveen's Marriage

In early 1967, we received a message from my sister-in-law, Kaushalaya Behanji, that a nephew (Rajinder) of her son-in-law (Tilak Raj Khanna) had come from Germany on a holiday and was keen to get married. If we felt interested we could go to Delhi and meet the young man. Rajinder Kumar Khanna was a qualified architect from the J.J. School of Arts and had a further degree from England. His father was in Government service and lived in his own house in Green Park. We were keen to settle Praveen, so we both went to Delhi and also asked Praveen to come to Delhi. We all met and gave ourselves a couple of days to think, and as both sides felt satisfied, the engagement took place, giving us exactly two weeks to arrange the wedding. I stayed on in Delhi with Sarlabibi, and the marriage took place from her house in Defence Colony on 14 February. I was keen that Praveen should complete her MA before she joined R.K. He readily agreed because in any case getting the necessary paper work done from Germany would take sometime. Soon after the wedding he left for Germany, and Praveen went back to Agra and I spent a little time in Agra before she left for Germany in April. We did not see her for the next two years till they returned to Delhi in 1969. Savita, our first granddaughter, was born in July 1968. Their decision to return to India was very pleasing for us and we all went to Delhi to receive them on their arrival. I had a great thrill when I took one year old Savita in my arms. She was a lovely baby.

In 1967 I returned to Patiala. I suddenly felt very tired. Too much had happened between August 1965 and February 1967. I then had a full grip over this demanding period. Physically I was quite unwell also, and felt that I needed a complete rest. N.P. could not see any reason for me to feel so low, when I had put up such a brave face when he left the Air Force. Now when I think back I feel it was the reaction of the tense period I went through when I feared that if N.P. went into a depression, life would become impossible. However, after a while I started feeling better, particularly after Pavan got his commission in the Indian Army in December 1967. It was a great day for N.P. and me to go to Dehra Dun and attend the passing out parade of our son who was only 19 years old.

Indu finished her Indian School Leaving Certificate and went to the Government College in Chandigarh to do her BA in English. She had very good marks and entry to the college was no problem, but getting a seat in the hostel was difficult. She was able to get in because English Honours was not available in any college in Patiala. So now we were by ourselves in Patiala. In 1969 we received a telegram from Jaipur that Raja Bhai Sahib was ill and in hospital. N.P. flew to Jaipur, and invited both Chandji and Bhai Sahib to come and live with us in Patiala once he felt a little better. We had a huge house and could easily spare three rooms, a bathroom and another room which could be turned into a kitchen. Chandji was keen to go to Delhi where her brother had a furnished rented flat which was lying vacant, because he had shifted to his son in Calcutta. But both Raja Bhai Sahib and Panditji, a gentleman who taught scriptures to Chandji and was held in great regard, thought differently and preferred that they should avail of the invitation that we extended. Raja Bhai Sahib realized that Chandji by herself would not be able to look after him. So they arrived, bag and baggage, and settled down nicely in the three rooms and were very happy to walk about in the large compound for some months. Rajaji kept quite well, but was under the supervision of a doctor all the time.

In February, N.P. and I went to attend the weddings of my nephews Surrinder and Narinder, and returned in the first week of March. After a few days, N.P. went to the Rashtriya Indian Military College (RIMC) for the annual reunion. He was to be away for three days and Pavan was with us for his annual leave. Soon after N.P. left we found Rajaji's health deteriorating and the doctor suggested that he should be shifted to the hospital. N.P. rang up to say that he was going away with friends for another day, but I insisted that he returned immediately because Rajaji seemed to be sinking. N.P. came back immediately. The following day Rajaji was shifted to the hospital, and he passed away after another 24 hours on 20 March 1970. Rajaji not having any children, Pavan performed all the ceremonies that were the duty of a son, including lighting the funeral pyre. He did all that was expected of a traditional Hindu and won a place in Chandji's heart who treated him like a son, and when the time came for her to be taken care of, both Pavan and Shyama (his wife) rose to the occasion and every care was given to her before she passed away.

Chandji continued to stay with us till December 1970, but then expressed a desire to shift to Delhi, basically because she needed spiritual stimulus, which only Panditji could give. We did not try to keep her back, but assured her that whenever she desired to return to us, she would always be most welcome. She stayed in Delhi by herself till 1990 and we would always look her up whenever we went to Delhi. She was a woman of great courage and managed her own affairs without any assistance. We did not worry as she lived in a very secure colony of Shri Ram Institute in Old Delhi and had several neighbours who had our address and telephone number in case of any emergency.

Now when I think back, I feel that had we gone to Bombay, we could never have been able to give the love and affection and care Raja Bhai Sahib got from us. And soon after his death we shifted to Chandigarh, and never had a house like the one in Patiala. It was God's wish that he should have such a good end, that He created such circumstances for us. Had Rajaji been taken ill when we ourselves were living in an annexure and looking for a job, we could have done nothing.

Ashok Sodhi got married and was posted to Patiala. We welcomed the new bride Punam. It was a pleasure to meet them. They were allotted Government accommodation and used to come over occasionally. I have always found them both very affectionate and respectful.

In 1971 we got the sad news of the sudden death of H.K., Nirmala's husband. The whole family had gone to visit my brother in Calcutta, where H.K. died of a massive heart attack. We rushed to Agra. It was a very untimely death. He was hardly fifty-five. He had put in earnest hard work for nearly twenty years and was able to rehabilitate himself and be comfortable. At last prosperity and success were at his door step when he passed away. Credit must be given to his son, Madhu, and his wife, Milan, and younger brother, Arvind, who were able to hold the reins of the business and were able to make the enterprise a big success.

We Shift to Chandigarh

Soon after we came to Patiala, the new states of Haryana and Himachal Pradesh were created. Chandigarh continued to be the capital of both Punjab and Haryana. Air Marshal Harjinder Singh now had to choose one of the states and he opted for Haryana. After sometime, he found that he needed a competent man as his assistant, and in September 1971 he rang up N.P. and asked him to come to Chandigarh and meet him in his office. N.P. was now the chief officer in civil aviation Punjab, and seemed a little reluctant to meet him in the office. I persuaded him to go, for after all he had proved to be a good friend and was instrumental in getting us this job, so N.P. went and met him. Harjinder introduced him to the Chief Secretary of Haryana. Privately he told him that he would like N.P. to join him. N.P. came home and mentioned this to me. The following day we got news that Harjinder had died of a heart attack. We naturally rushed for the funeral and the fourth day ceremony when the Chief Secretary offered N.P. the position of Aviation Advisor, Haryana, with much better terms then he had in Punjab. I was now keen that he should accept this offer for two reasons; first, because the terms were much better and secondly, because Indu was in a boarding college, and when she finished her B.A, she would have to be in Chandigarh for further studies.

Once Lahore became a part of Pakistan, a new city of Chandigarh was built on the foothills of the Shivalik range of the Himalayas, as the capital of East Punjab. A Swiss architect, Le Corbusier [50], designed it on the banks of the artificially-created Sukhna Lake. The city was built in sectors of various sizes: Government offices and Legislative Assemblies on one side, residential houses for the Governor and other senior officials on another. Similarly, for ordinary citizens, there were sectors with large and small plots. There were a few large avenues. Special attention was paid to the flora. Flowering trees were planted on both sides of the roads and when these Gul Mohars [51], Jacarandas, and Liburnums were in bloom, they presented a riot of colours which was very pleasing to the eye. In the heart of the city there was a large space which served as a walking area where a beautiful rose garden was created. Two large Government Colleges were set up for women and men near the University Campus, and a whole sector was allocated to the Postgraduate Institute for Research, and for a hospital.

When the Punjab was further bifurcated into Haryana and Himachal, Chandigarh, which was a Union Territory, continued to serve as the capaital of Haryana also. A big township of Panchkula came up in Haryana adjoining Chandigarh, and an Army station was built called Chandi Mandir.

N.P. gave two months' notice to the Punjab Government and was released on 30 November, and joined Haryana on 1 December 1971. On 3 December 1971, Pakistan started bombing Chandigarh, Agra, and Delhi simultaneously, signifying the beginning of the 1971 war with Pakistan, which ended after 14 days. All this time I was by myself in Patiala, dealing with blackouts and packing. Fortunately I did not know that Pavan was also in the war on the eastern front in East Pakistan, otherwise I would have had further worries. This war led to the creation of another independent state, Bangladesh. By the end of December, N.P. was able to get a house on rent in Section 11 and I shifted to Chandigarh.

Life in Chandigarh was pleasant. N.P. was happy with his job which was interesting. He was dealing with Chief Ministers, Ministers of Haryana, and the

Governor who were the main people using the aircraft. Indu's college was just five minutes' walk from our house. We of course joined the Club and found it much better then Patiala.

On their return to India, R.K. and Praveen lived in Green Park and R.K. was employed by Kotharis, a well known firm of Architects. Praveen had a lot of free time and she started teaching in General Raj's school which was just across the road. After a while, the General, whom we had known in Wellington, and had started this school after retiring, just mentioned to Praveen that if she had a Bachelor degree in Education (a teaching qualification), her pay would be much better. Praveen liked the idea; it was only a one-year course, and if she could do it from Chandigarh, it would be very convenient. I also endorsed the idea, there were enough holidays for her to be able to go to Delhi whenever she pleased, for it was only a five hour journey. R.K. agreed as Praveen was not running the house, they were staying with his parents. Indu had just finished her BA and so both the sisters did their Bachelors of Education together. Little Savita, who was now about four years old, was going to a nursery school close to our house. The main thing I remember of this period is that when she came home from school she refused to have lunch with us and wanted to wait till Praveen returned at about 3.30 pm. So I would give her a plate of potato chips, which she readily accepted, and would do a lot of painting on her own and did not bother us at all.

Indu had cultivated quite a few friends when she was in the hostel and during this time the house buzzed. I was kept quite busy baking biscuits and cakes for the family as well as her friends. In short it was a happy time. In April 1973, both Praveen and Indu finished their BEd. Praveen topped the class in practical, and Indu in theory.

While Praveen and Indu were studying, Tara's husband Ravi Sahney passed away after a serious illness, on Diwali day 1972. This was a great tragedy for her and the entire family. She was very young and had been married for only eight years. There were two young sons. Tara threw herself into her work and lived for several years with her in-laws. She built her own house and moved there in 1983. Her boys Rajeev and Naveen grew up there, and are very caring towards their mother. They are both pursuing successful careers in finance and banking. I attended both their weddings in due course.

Pavan's Marriage

In early September 1973, we got a letter from Pavan who was in Pune, that he had met a very nice Maharashtrian girl, Shyama Kher, and he would like us to meet her. Both N.P. and I were very excited and happy, and I wrote back to say that as long as the girl came from a respectable family and was educated, her being Maharashtrian would not be a hurdle. Before giving our final consent we would like to meet the young lady and her mother (Pavan had already told us that the father had died and the mother was working). As luck would have it, N.P. had to go to Bombay for some official work. I suggested that it would be a good opportunity for him to go to Pune and meet the young girl. N.P. agreed but insisted that I should also go with him, because then we could take a final decision. So we sent a telegram to Pavan saying that we were both coming to Pune and it would be nice if we could meet the mother also. While N.P. had to spend a couple of days in Bombay, I went to Pune a day earlier and from my compartment while the train was still moving on the platform I saw a tall, fair, striking young lady standing by herself on the platform, and the thought came to me that this must be the young lady I was going to meet. My guess was right. The following day, N.P. also arrived and we both met her. Shyama struck us as a girl full of confidence, well spoken and educated. We knew that Pavan was really keen to marry her and was only looking for our approval and blessings, which we readily gave. The next day we met Mrs Kher and the engagement took place. I had taken a diamond ring and a beautiful sari for Shyama. Gifts were exchanged and the engagement took place in the house of Dr Kale, a cousin of Shyama.

I invited Mrs Kher to Chandigarh so as to give her a fair idea of the home her daughter was marrying into. The date of the wedding was fixed for 16 January 1974. We decided to have the wedding in Delhi, where the Khers would have to treat us like a local *Barat* and we would take about eighty people for dinner, as there was a restriction imposed by the Government that no cereal was to be served if there were more than 100 guests at a wedding. The other alternative was to have the wedding in Nagpur where they would have had to put up all the guests from our side. Mrs Kher agreed to have the wedding in Delhi, as her brother-in-law, a Mr. Paranjape, was posted in Delhi as a member of the Railway Board. She could have the wedding from his house which was very centrally located. This made it very convenient for us also as most of our relatives were in Delhi, and a few who had to come to Delhi were easily accommodated with other members of the family.

We had not been very long in Chandigarh and N.P. was keen to have a simple wedding. We had a lovely *Satsang* [52] and ladies music on the morning of 15 January, and then N.P., Indu, Pavan, and I set out for Delhi by car – we spent a night at Uchana Lake – and reached Delhi on 16 January morning. We had the *Sehra Bandhi* at Sarlabibi's place. This is a religious function held in the bridegroom's house before leaving for the bride's house. The bridegroom generally sits on a much decorated horse, and the elders make him wear some flowers on his forehead attached to his turban. It is now not possible for the bridegroom to ride all the way, but the ceremony still persists, when the sisters of the groom feed the horse with delicacies and the sisters-in-law put a little *surma* [53] in the groom's eyes to wish him a safe journey. The parents then give presents to them. This custom is really practiced only in the Punjab. Basically it means that the womenfolk wish him a safe journey, because the women did not accompany the Barat (the bridegroom's party consisting of men only). All that has now changed, but the ceremony is still held. We then went to the National Sports Club, which was considered quite prestigious, with beautiful lawns and halls. Members could book it for weddings for themselves or relations. Sarlabibi's son, Rajen, had also got married there and we had liked the place very much. We reached the Club, the wedding ceremony was performed, a very good dinner was laid by the Khers, and after dinner we took the *Doli* to Haryana Bhavan where N.P. had booked a couple of rooms. In older days the bride was brought home in a palanquin called *Doli*. Now a car is generally decorated with flowers and both the bride and groom sit together and return to the bridegroom's house, but it is still called *Doli*. The next morning we had lunch with the Paranjapes, and returned to Chandigarh. We had a tea reception on 19 January at the Club, where we entertained about 200 guests.

Pavan and Shyama returned to Pune and set up their home. It was a delightful wedding, everything was very nice and dignified, and I think both sides were quite happy and there was no sense of anxiety on either side because both Pavan and Shyama had known each other and wanted the union. We met them again after a year, when Pavan had annual leave, and we were delighted to see our little granddaughter Radhika who was born on 29 December 1974 in Pune. Shyama's mother, Mrs. Kher, was with them for the delivery. Soon after, Pavan was posted in Chandi Mandir and they stayed with us for a few months till he was allotted a house. I had never seen N.P. so happy as he was with Radhika. He could spend hours playing with her and she was very happy spending time with us. I think he was too busy with his work and career when his own children were young. It was always left to me to attend their school functions or meet teachers or arrange parties for their friends. I realized then the value of a Punjabi saying that one enjoys the interest more than the capital.

This was made even more obvious when Praveen and R.K. went to Iran in the seventies. That was the time when there were lots of disturbances there, and Praveen had to return with Savita and left her with us. So Savita joined school in Chandigarh. R.K. and Praveen also returned, but soon after R.K. went to Lagos on a new assignment and Praveen followed. She returned in June or July 1979. Praveen was now expecting her second child after a gap of almost eleven years. Savita needed ortho-dentistry for her teeth. I give full marks to both Savita and N.P. for taking a step, which needed years of regular visits to the dentist. Savita was extremely co-operative and never complained. Even when I could see her quite uncomfortable and inquired she would just say *"I am alright"*. Getting a tooth extracted at the age of eleven was no joke. I admired her for her determination and N.P. would never change the appointment and would forgo his club and bridge but never be late for the dentist. All this trouble was worthwhile, for this further enhanced Savita's good looks.

I have always admired this quality of dogged perseverance in Savita. She has a way of getting what she wants in life. She did her fashion designing course from the prestigious National Institute of Fashion Technology (NIFT), which is an extremely demanding course. Even after her marriage with a very supportive husband, she manages the house, her child, and her work very efficiently and successfully.

Coming back to our life in Chandigarh, I was kept busy with lots of cultural and social activities. There was the *Mangal Satsang* [54], which was held once a week every Tuesday in each members house turn by turn, where a *Havan* [55] was conducted, followed by a small prayer, a few *Bhajans* and then a discourse by a member who was well versed in any religious subject. Generally a book was followed and over the years we were able to study the Ramayana by Tulsidas, the Gita, Yoga Darshan and one or two Upanishads. I also joined the blood bank. Chandigarh was a town in which selling or buying of blood was not allowed. So voluntary blood donations had to be monitored and there was a group of ladies who would go to colleges and try to get young people involved to donate blood regularly, with the assurance that in case they or their nearest kin ever needed blood it would be provided without asking any return. We attended blood donation camps and wrote articles on the subject to make people aware of the danger of buying contaminated blood. I also got involved in a musical group, where we had a few very good singers, all housewives, and we would meet once a month and have a nice musical session. I did not sing at all but organized different festivals with appropriate music for the occasion. This group called the *'Prerana'* became very popular and at least two or three of our members encouraged a few children whom they started teaching. Their talent gave them a fair amount of extra income as music schools were still rare in Chandigarh. Having lived in Bengal, I was always interested in Dramatics, and with my association with the Inner Wheel Club, I was able to produce children's plays with the assistance of *'Prerana ladies'*.

I was elected the President of the Thursday Club, which consisted of about 100 ladies. Meetings were held every Thursday morning in the Sector 9 Club. We had at least two cultural programmes a month. Besides all this, there was the Chandigarh Club where both N.P. and I went every evening for a game of bridge and rummy.

As time went by, Indu finished her MA and MEd. She won a scholarship to America sponsored by the Rotary Club. Her subject was teaching English as a foreign language: the scholarship was for nine months, but the course was for a year. So we decided to pay for the last three months to enable her to get the degree. She was in Vermont for a year (1977-78). While returning home she chose to visit the United Nations (UN) in New York and managed to get an interview a day before she left for India. Within a month, she received a cable asking her to join the UN within a week. Hectic activities took place, several telephone calls with the UN ensued. Getting a visa was no joke, but UN assured us that she would get the visa without delay as they had informed the visa section in Delhi. So off she went again. This was in 1978.

Soon after Indu left for America in 1977, I happened to be in Delhi attending Vinod Sodhi's wedding when we received news that my brother Sarupji was coming to Delhi with his entire family. He was very unwell and was admitted to the All India Medical Institute for treatment. It was obviously something very serious. After all the investigations were done and the treatment had just started, he died suddenly. Besides his immediate family, all his brothers and sisters were with him: Devji and Nirmala came from Agra, Shaktiji and Savitri came from Darjeeling, thus he met the whole family before he passed away. He was only 66 years old and we all felt his loss very much. I rarely had an occasion to visit Calcutta after my father's death, but I am very glad that all my three children visited Calcutta during my brother's lifetime and were able to see the house where I spent my growing up years. I met my niece Saroj's two lovely daughters in England when I was passing through England in 1997. My sister-in-law Lalo Bibi passed away a couple of years ago, but I was unable to go to Calcutta on account of my own ill health. Now my nephew Raghu has given up the Mandeville Gardens house, and shifted to Delhi, so my connection with Calcutta has become more tenuous.

When N.P. was 66 years old he was contemplating retirement. As the time approached, he found it difficult to close up the house and shift to Pavan who was posted in Pune. All his friends advised N.P. to live independently as long as possible, and suddenly he also started thinking like them. After retiring, we went to Kasauli for a holiday which was a favourite resort for both of us.

Kasauli is a little hill station, a few miles off the main Kalka-Simla road. It is an Army cantonment with a small population, catering basically to the needs of the Army. It has houses which are well separated, and there are no big hotels or restaurants, as it has never become a tourist resort. There is a Club, which included a few rooms for accommodating the families of British officers whenever they were in India, and some small bungalows across the road where those families who wished could cook their own food. In Sanawar, close to Kasauli, there was a school for the British children. When the British left, this school became a very popular public school. Kasauli has never lost its charm, unlike other hill stations such as Mussoorie and Darjeeling. Kasauli continues to be a military cantonment which retired Army personnel find very attractive on account of its moderate climate and peaceful atmosphere. In fact it is quite a favourite place for retired Army officers who use the Army holiday homes. Kasauli is about two hours' drive from Chandigarh and N.P. loved running up there for long weekends.

We shifted to Sector 9 in Chandigarh, in an annex consisting of two bedrooms, with a nice courtyard, one in front and another at the back. In the main house in front lived Mr. and Mrs. Mehra, who turned out to be very good neighbours. We shifted because our landlords in Sector 11 were pestering us to leave, and since we were planning to live in Kasauli for at least six months, we did not mind shifting into a smaller place closer to Savita's school. We decided to put Savita in the Convent boarding school, as we were planning a long stay in Kasauli. She went to Lagos for her summer holidays, and after a couple of months in the boarding, she preferred to come back to us when we returned from Kasauli, and stayed with us till she finished her tenth grade in 1984.

While still in Chandigarh we received a telephone from K.P. informing us that his wife Rajan was critically ill. N.P. decided to leave for Delhi the next morning and I accompanied him. We went straight to the hospital with flowers. We crept into the room quietly and found her looking extremely weak and frail. She gave us a smile and held my hand with as much strength as she could muster. I was deeply moved by her gesture and felt only affection and compassion. There were tears in my eyes as she was trying to thank us for visiting her. We returned to Chandigarh the following day as Praveen was expecting her child to be born soon.

A few days later Rajan passed away, and we later went to Ambala for a day where her son Vijai and Doreen had the 13th day ceremony for his mother, with a *"path"* from *"Durbar Sahib"*[56] as Rajan was born a Sikh.

Prashant was born on 6 December 1979. We took Praveen to the hospital at about 4 am and I stayed there while N.P. returned home to be with Savita. I waited there till about 11 am but there was no sign of the child arriving. At about 1 pm, the nurse walked out with a big smile saying that a bonny son was born. We were all very happy because this completed her family of a daughter and a son. R.K.'s mother and sister came the next day from Delhi to see her grandson, a Khanna boy, and I could see how thrilled and happy she was to hold that child in her arms. Prashant always had a great affection for his granny and still has her picture by his bedside. He helped to look after her in her last illness. Prashant later graduated in Commerce and then completed a two year course in computer studies. He is now working with General Electric. He is an ambitious young man, full of life and energy.

Praveen returned to Nigeria and both R.K. and she visited us once or twice during the next four years. Prashant's early childhood was spent in Nigeria. We saw more of Prashant when the family returned to India for good in 1989 and stayed with us in Delhi for about six months before they bought their flat in Noida.

We Sell Our House

After retiring we had decided to be on our own, but we found that the pension from the Air Force and the rent from the house were not enough to maintain the standard of living that we were used to. Both N.P. and I came from secure homes, had a good start in life, and did not have to save money to make our homes comfortable. N.P. got the first jolt when his father lost the lands in the Punjab after Partition. Once we had a little money and land was allotted to us in Defence Colony Delhi, we built the ground floor of our house. At that time we had to take a loan of about nine thousand rupees and belonging to the old school of thought that running a debt was a bad thing, I decided to sell some of the gold I possessed which was indeed a very foolish thing to do. The rest of the loan was cleared with the rent. In 1962 we added a couple of rooms upstairs and the little bungalow turned into a lovely four bedroom house which could now be rented out to senior executives or industrialists. The rent almost doubled.

This time the rooms were built on a loan which would be paid off in a few years from the rent we received, but I was wiser and did not volunteer to part with any more of my jewellery.

We received the next jolt when N.P. retired from the Air Force. He got his pension commuted and received money from the Provident Fund. This money proved to be very useful for the eight months when he was without a job. He had to travel a fair amount and I insisted that he should travel first class, which we had always done. In the Armed Forces we had a concession that we paid a second class fare and travelled first class. Now that concession was not there, but I felt that if he did not travel in comfort he would get further depressed and that was something I wanted to avoid at all cost. Closing the house in Kanpur and shifting to Patiala on our own expense was also a drain on our finances. A fair amount of money thus got spent.

So when N.P. retired from the Haryana Government, he suddenly found that our income was not enough. Prices were rising by leaps and bounds, but we did not feel the pinch as the Haryana Government salary made us quite comfortable. What we had not catered for was inflation. He never thought it possible to reduce his expenses, so he started thinking of ways and means of increasing his income. Rents were also rising and

N.P. asked the tenant to increase the rental payments. The tenant agreed to raise the rent by a very small sum which made no sense. N.P. then requested him to vacate the house. This request fell on deaf ears, but he indicated that he would be interested in buying the house if we ever wanted to sell it. If we had vacant possession of the house the price would have been fantastic but unfortunately we knew that the tenants would never vacate. The landlord could get the house only if he was going to occupy it himself. N.P. was not inclined to get into litigation and spend time on court hearings and engaging lawyers who would charge fantastic fees for appearing in court for every hearing. So he decided to sell the house to the tenant if he would give us a good price. So a beautiful house was sold, and today the price is at least twenty times more. But still at that time it suited us to sell it, for the return we got from the sum was almost double the rent. Not having any business acumen, we were not able to comprehend that the prices would go on rising and that we had thrown away the goose that was laying the golden eggs. I do not absolve myself of blame, for I knew what was happening. To be very frank I never looked upon it as my future home. I never spent even a day there, we never had a proper house warming party, the house had been rented even before it was completed. To me it was like an investment that gave us a good return, so if selling it was beneficial then it was alright. After all, people buy and sell shares, they do not have any sentimental value for them. I know that both Shyama and Indu felt the loss of the house very much and I myself regretted a foolish decision. Now I don't feel so bad because all three of my children have got their own properties and are living in them and enjoying them. N.P lived only four years after selling the house. I at least have the satisfaction that his last years were spent in comfort and he did not have the worries of litigation or any financial stringency.

In January 1980 we attended Arvind and Sudha's wedding in Agra. Shyama and Radhika came with us and so did Prakash Behanji who was visiting us. It was a grand wedding. Since this wedding was held after H.K.'s death, both Madhu and Milan were very keen to have it on a lavish scale, as their own wedding had been. Although Nirmala was not feeling very well, she attended the wedding. After her husband's death in 1971, Nirmala had stopped attending all other social functions and weddings and spent much more time in Mount Abu at the Sanyas Ashram. Soon after the wedding, her younger son Som decided to become a sanyasi and gave up all his rights on the property. He was given the name Swami Swayam Prakash Giri. He took the Diksha[57] from Mahamandaleshwara Swami

Maheshananda Giri who was the Head of the Order of Dakshinamurti of Varanasi. This was the first time in the history of our family that a family member gave up the world and accepted Sanyas. Today he is a very learned Sanskrit scholar of India and has several books to his credit.

FAMILY PHOTO ON THE OCCASION OF
ARVIND'S WEDDING, 1980

FRONT ROW (LEFT TO RIGHT) : ARVIND,
SUDHA, NIRMALA

LADIES IN SECOND ROW: SAVITRI, SARLA,
BASANT, KAMLA

MEN IN BACK ROW: SHAKTI, NARINJAN,
SOM PRAKESH, DEV, ARJUN

NIRMALA AND BASANT AT THE
CHATTARPUR FARM ON BASANT'S
BIRTHDAY, 2000

Trip to Vaishno Devi

In 1980, Indu came home from America on a holiday for a month. She expressed a desire to go to Vaishno Devi, a very famous place of pilgrimage in the foothills of Kashmir. I readily agreed and we went to Jammu by car. On the way we passed a township called Dasuya a few miles away from Jullunder. I knew that all the refugees from Ghartal (the village my Father came from in Punjab) were allotted land in Dasuya, which meant that lots of Puri families were settled there. I mentioned this to Indu and we proceeded to Jammu. The next morning we went to Katra and then on to Vaishno Devi on horses. It was not a very difficult journey and there were hundreds of devotees going up and coming back with the chant *Jai Mata Di* [58]. We were able to go through a very small cave with water flowing right up to our knees, the path was through a very narrow tunnel. It is said that with the grace of the Mother every one can go through it and have a *darshan* [59] where a priest is sitting and gives the *Prasad* [60]. We were very happy that there was no delay to get the *darshan* for sometimes one has to wait several hours if not a full day before one takes one's turn. We got back to Jammu the same evening and left for Chandigarh soon after breakfast the next day, After a while, N.P. asked us *"Where would you like to have lunch"?* Very spontaneously I said *"Let's have it in Dasuya"*. N.P. then laughingly addressed Indu and said *"My dear, you are visiting the land of your Nankas. All your Mammas*[61] *will be there to receive you"*. I was feeling a little sentimental and did not quite enjoy the tone in which it was said, but I kept quiet. When we reached Dasuya, N.P. stopped the car near a wine shop which had a Dhaba close by: a wayside eating place for travellers, particularly for bus drivers, who want a quick meal. He ordered lunch to be brought to us in the car in *thalis*[62] while he had a beer in the wine shop. There he got in conversation with the shop-keeper and mentioned to him that his father-in-law also came from Ghartal. N.P. came back and we left.

The food was rather nice and I asked N.P. how much it cost. N.P. very sheepishly answered *"The shop-keeper did not permit me to pay, he said that after all a sister was visiting us"*. I was very touched for if I had some sentimental feeling for this place, there was someone else who appreciated and reciprocated the same sentiment. It is an incident I will always cherish. *"Thank you brother for your hospitality"*. I think N.P. also appreciated the gesture by not insisting on paying for the food. It is a very pleasant memory and speaks highly of an old tradition that the daughters of a village were treated as their own daughters and sisters by other villagers.

Indu returned from New York after working for the United Nations for three years. She joined us in Kasauli for a short holiday and then went to Delhi and stayed with Kay and G.P. She took up an appointment with the United Nations Children's Fund (UNICEF) in September 1981.

Tega's Death and my Trip to Pune

In January 1982 we received the sad news of Tega's (Rupa's husband) death in Algiers, where he had been on an assignment for Engineers India. Both N.P. and I rushed to Agra where my brother Devji lived. The next news that we received was that the family with the body were being flown to Bombay, as Tega's father lived in his farm house in Pune. Pavan was posted in Pune, so we sent him a telegram that a whole group of people from Agra would be reaching Pune via Bombay. There was enough time to reach Bombay by train and so my sister-in-law, her two daughters and Kay and Nita, Madhu (Nirmala's son) and I left the following day. My brother Devji was in very delicate health (he had angina) and was inconsolable. I had full confidence in Shyama that she would take very good care of all the people who went but I thought I would be helpful not only to her but be a support to my sister-in-law also. In Bombay we were received by

Kay's friend, who came with us in her own car, so we hired one taxi and left for Pune very late at night after receiving Rupa and her three children. Tega's father had made all the arrangements for the body to be taken to the Sasson hospital in Pune.

We reached Pavan's flat in the College of Military Engineering at about 2 am to find a big lock on Pavan's main door. We were in two cars and when the people on the ground floor saw the cars full of women folk, they opened the door to see what was happening. When I introduced myself they very kindly invited me in and told us that Pavan was away to Bombay on temporary duty and Shyama and Radhika had taken the opportunity of spending a few days with her sister. Their maid lived in the servant quarters, so the officer went and called her. She told us that the keys of the house were with Colonel Kher who lived close by. I left with her to fetch the keys. The neighbour's wife very kindly made tea and served it with biscuits. Fortunately I knew Colonel Kher from Chandigarh and on ringing the bell, before opening the door he enquired who I was. When I told him, he quickly opened the door and ushered me into the drawing room. He gave me the keys and volunteered to inform Pavan early next morning. I now knew how useful my trip proved, otherwise my sister-in-law and her daughters would have been extremely inconvenienced. As we opened the house, we found it all in good order. We got into the beds and Madhu made himself comfortable on the drawing room carpet. Early morning there was a knock at the door, the people downstairs sent us some bread, butter and milk. After a little while, Surekha, Colonel Kher's wife, sent us a big dish of *Poha* [63]. However sad one may be, hunger has a way of getting the better of one. Since we had gone without dinner, this food was most welcome. We were getting ready to go to the farm as early as possible because we did not know when the funeral would take place. The kitchen was very well set and we had no problem in finding tea and sugar. Everybody was most appreciative that the house without the mistress around was so well organized. I gave the maid some money and told her to arrange lunch for us. We left the house at about 9.30 am. Pavan and Shyama reached home at about 3 pm, and then came straight to the farm and were able to attend the funeral. Kay's friend and Madhu were keen to get back to Bombay, so Pavan also returned with them. Shyama looked after us for the next ten days and everybody was highly appreciative of her hospitality and good house keeping.

Till Death Do Us Part

In September 1982, Pavan came to Chandigarh for a couple of days and very excitedly he said *"Guess where I am posted?"* I replied, *"You must give us some clue, is it a hot or cold place?"* *"Cold"*. *"Is it somewhere in Kashmir?"*. *"No"* came the answer. *"Is it a foreign country?"* I said. *"Yes"*, he replied. *"Are they sending you to Canada?"* *"No"*, he said. *"They certainly can't send you to the Arctic"*, I said. *"Well, they are sending me to the Antarctic"*, he replied with a big grin. This was the second expedition to the Antarctic; the first one lasted only twelve days, a sort of a recce. This one was to last for eight weeks and the time of going and returning would be another eight weeks. Thus the whole time away from home would be about four months. There was a lot of excitement, and the whole of India was talking about it. He left in December 1982 and returned after a successful trip in March 1983. Both N.P. and I were very happy that our son had been a member of this successful expedition, and were even happier to know that Shyama was pregnant and the baby was due in December.

In June 1983, Indu came across an advertisement that an executive post was available in the British High Commission. Indu applied and was invited to appear for a written test and then an interview. There were a thousand applicants. She got through both exams and was duly appointed as Senior Development Officer in the British High Commission in September 1983. R.K. and Praveen were well settled in Lagos and Savita was with us. All was well, or so we thought.

We did not go to Kasauli in 1983, as in the previous year N.P. got a severe bout of diarrhoea which needed drastic treatment. Once we returned to Chandigarh he was alright, so we thought that the water had perhaps not suited him, and if we liked we could always run up for the weekend if we wanted to. However I noticed that slowly and steadily N.P. was losing weight and eating less. I also found him quite critical of the food served and he would find some excuse to eat less. The more I tried to improve the quality of food, he became worse. I then suggested that he should consult a doctor, but he refused. *"There is nothing wrong with me, only the food is not nice."* In May he got a little diarrhoea again and he went to the doctor who put him through several tests which did not show any significant defect.

I did suggest once that he should go to the Military Hospital, but he did not seem inclined. I also did not insist because I did not want him to think that I wanted to save money and get free treatment to which we were entitled. He now started spending more time in bed. I tried to persuade him to go out for a while but he simply refused. I noticed that he no longer relished his evening drink. I consulted the doctor and he said "*A peg or two in the evening would be a very good thing*". We never really know what to ask from God. I always used to think what a wonderful day it would be if N.P. said "*I don't need a drink*". Well when the day arrived, with tears in my eyes I was trying to persuade him to have a sip, and he was refusing. "*I don't want it, I have no taste in my mouth*". This went on for a couple of months till on 26 September he came from the bathroom and said that instead of stool he had passed only blood.

I rang up the doctor. He asked me to get a test done and he would come and see him in the afternoon. I rang up Dr Chopra who was a very good friend of ours. He was not at home, but his wife said that she would fix up an appointment and within a few minutes she came over and took us to Dr Talwar for the test. Once the test was over I asked the doctor what exactly was the matter. He seemed a little reluctant to say anything. "*Your doctor will tell you*". On my insisting and saying that we were by ourselves and I had to depend on friends, he said *"This is no time to be by your selves. Where are your children?"*. "My daughter is in Delhi and my son is in Pune", I replied. *"Why don't you go to Delhi. He needs hospitalization and you will get excellent treatment in the Military Hospital. Don't waste time. He is still moving around"*. I thanked him and returned home. I put N.P. in bed and rushed to my cousin Brigadier Kochar and told him about the conversation with the doctor. Brigadier Kochar then suggested that we should leave for Delhi the next afternoon, and he would go by the early morning bus and arrange a room for us in the Military Hospital. I asked Surrinder my nephew who was posted in Chandigarh to arrange the air tickets. The Mehras were very helpful and volunteered that Savita should stay with them as she would have the company of their two daughters. Surrinder informed Indu the next morning that we would be reaching Delhi. It so happened that Indu had returned from a tour to Calcutta the previous evening and decided to spend the night with my sister in Safdarjang Enclave, instead of going to New Friends Colony which was much further away from the airport. Gautam and Indu, Brigadier Kochar and his son were at the airport to receive us. We had had a very comfortable journey and N.P. was admitted to the Intensive Care Unit of the Military Hospital.

The next morning I asked Indu to go to the Army Headquarters and meet the engineer-in-chief and request him to ask Pavan to come to Delhi as his father was seriously ill. Indu went and met the General who rang up Pune to get in touch with Pavan who was then a Major. Within ten minutes he received a message that Pavan had already left for Delhi on duty and would reach in the evening. This came as a very pleasant surprise to us. On reporting at Army Headquarters the following morning he was told about N.P.'s illness and he arrived at the hospital at about 11 am. It was a great relief to have both Pavan and Indu with me.

Indu and I were staying with Kay and G.P. who gave us utmost care and attended to all our needs. They put their chauffeur-driven car at our disposal and Arjun who was leaving for Kashmir left his car with Pavan who was staying with Sarlaji. Both my brother and bhabi and Nirmala came from Agra. My brother and bhabi also returned from Kashmir. N.P.'s own brother K.P. was in Delhi and N.P. had the pleasure of meeting so many of his friends and relations who were in Delhi. He was particularly pleased when Swami Maheshanandaji came to see him and bless him. I can still remember the beautiful expression that N.P. had, an expression of humility, respect and happiness put together. N.P.'s condition grew worse day by day. He was put on nasal feeding, then on blood transfusion, and ultimately the doctors suggested that they could try dialysis which would certainly be very painful, but they were not sure how much it would help. Both Pavan and I agreed that he should not be put to any further pain.

He was talking to us till about 6 October and then gradually fell into a coma and breathed his last on 9 October 1983, the third day of *Navratras* which are considered very auspicious. Pavan, Indu and I were by his side and I could feel his lips move as I was saying "*Om, Om*"[64] very loudly.

The funeral was to take place the next morning at the Lodi cremation ground. At about 11 am, friends and relations, brother officers and colleagues, were all waiting with flowers and wreaths to pay their last respects with tearful eyes. When I saw his face in the cremation ground I was absolutely stunned. His face was looking as it did at the age of forty five: it was full and not the shrunken old face of the previous evening – his face was swollen a little which gave it the fullness of youth - and he had a lovely crop of grey hair. There was a peaceful expression on his face, as if he was in a deep sleep. Pavan performed the last rites.

We got in touch with Shyama and I told her not to come. She was then seven months pregnant. I promised her that I would send Pavan back immediately after the thirteenth day prayer meeting. We had the fourth day ceremony in Delhi. Telephones were not as efficient as they are today and it took Indu a good ten days before she was able to get through to Lagos and inform Praveen. Pavan took two weeks leave, and Nirmala, Pavan and I left for Hardwar with the Ashes which we call *Phool* [65], which were consigned to the Ganga. Vijai Nair also joined us in Hardwar, having journeyed all the way from Ambala to be with us. In Chandigarh we held the thirteenth day prayer meeting where Praveen and Indu were also able to come. I was keen that Pavan should go back to Pune as Shyama was all alone, and Indu went back to the British High Commission as she had exhausted the leave that she was entitled to for her father's death. She was in a new job and I did not want to disturb her, but Praveen and Savita were with me for nearly a month.

Pavan had actually come to Delhi to work out the details of the third Antarctic Expedition. He had been chosen as the leader of the army contingent, which was going to build a permanent station (*Dakshin Gangotri*) in Antarctica. I was very perturbed and would have liked him to get out of the team. With N.P.'s death, everything seemed changed. Pavan felt that it was unfair to try and get out at this late stage. His sense of duty did not permit him even to mention that it was very inconvenient for him to leave his family. So we decided I would go to Pune just before he was leaving and stay there till the child was born and return to Chandigarh when Shyama's mother was able to come. Savita in the meantime would stay with Surrinder and Deepa. Their daughter Shivani also went to the convent and both the girls could go and come back together from school.

All this time I tried to keep up a brave face. Indu was in a new job. Praveen had already been to India twice and had left Prashant with R.K. in Lagos, so it was imperative for her to return to Lagos. Pavan had enough worries of his own, he was leaving behind his pregnant wife and was in charge of a very responsible assignment. A couple of days after my arrival in Pune, Praveen left for Lagos and Pavan for Goa to embark on his trip to Antarctica. During the day I would try to behave in a normal manner, but I would have sleepless nights and would weep quietly till I fell off to sleep out of sheer exhaustion.

Sometimes happy memories lingered. How encouraging N.P. had been when Nirmala and I started the little school for the street urchins. He cooperated fully when I was working with the refugee women. He would make the car available to me to go and buy the right quality of wool of fashionable colours and the latest pattern books. These books were written in English and I had to teach the women the designs and give the right measurements. Since most of them could knit very well, they picked up the designs quickly and turned out the most beautiful baby garments which found a ready market. Patiala and Chandigarh had more scope for cultural activities, with a lot of music and dancing thrown in. With the assistance of the Inner Wheel Club we put on several children's plays, which served as stepping stones for them to overcome stage fright, learn elocution, and improve their general knowledge. N.P. felt very happy and proud when I went as a volunteer to the blood donation group and spoke to students of different colleges, persuading them to donate blood. He was most cooperative when I put up a stall in the Red Cross fête which was held once a year. These happy memories would sometimes uplift my mood – but only for a short while.

How was it that I was not able to fathom the seriousness of his illness? The only answer I could find was that he never had any fever and did not complain of pain. When all the tests did not yield any specific cause I was concerned but not very worried. Ultimately when it was too late it was diagnosed as cancer of the gastro-intestinal tract. Had they found it earlier he could have undergone surgery but alas it was too late when they knew. He was indeed very fortunate that he did not suffer acute pain. God was merciful to grant him a good end.

All my life I had great regard for the teachings of the Gita and I thought I understood a fair amount. Its basic philosophy is that the soul is immortal, it never dies, the elements cannot destroy it, the soul only changes its body in which it resides and discards a worn out or a diseased body as one changes worn out or soiled clothes, without feeling any sorrow. One should not grieve in death which is inevitable, and what is inevitable should be accepted gracefully. The stress is on doing one's duty, leaving the rest to God. Never look for a reward for having done one's duty to the best of one's ability. I understood the philosophy alright but realized that though the soul may be imperishable, I had lost contact with it. I had lost him and the loss seemed immense. Reason said that he had enjoyed a good life and if he only had to linger on without getting well, it was better for him to go, but however hard I tried, I felt that I was a broken woman. My role as a daughter was finished when I lost my parents, but then I still had a life to look forward to with my husband and children. Now I had lost my husband and my role as wife was over. I realized that with time, which is a great healer, I may find some meaning in life with my loving children. I was now only a mother and grandmother.

I was still in that pensive mood when I got the news that N.P.'s elder brother K.P. had passed away. This meant that all the men of the Nair family of my generation had gone. Both the brothers-in-law and all the three brothers were fortunate; they had lived full lives. I always read with interest the seven stages of a man's life depicted by Shakespeare. Fortunately for them they passed through infancy, childhood, happy marriages, successful careers and retirement, but were spared the last stage of very old age when one is apt to lose one's physical and mental faculties and be like an infant once again needing constant looking after. Somehow I had a sense of relief that K.P. did not have to go through the last stage; perhaps it was because he had already lost his wife and was very independent by nature. Out of K.P.'s five children, three of them, Minnie (Uma), Chippy (Viveik), and Littlue have settled abroad, so I have not had any contact with them. Vinod and Brigadier Vijai Nair are here. I did meet Vinod occasionally in Delhi, but have had close contact with Vijai and Doreen who are now settled in Noida. They have only one son, Vijai Vir, who is the only Nair great-grandson of my father-in-law. He is not yet married, but I look forward to his wedding. Radhika and Malavika are my father-in-law's great-grand daughters.

Malavika is Born and Pavan returns from Antarctica

It was Radhika's birthday on 29 December 1983. Shyama had decided that there would be no party as her child was expected more or less on the same day. Besides I think she must have felt it was too soon to have a party after N.P.'s death. Radhika was nine years old, old enough to understand that her *Bade Daddy* (grandfather) as she called him was dead and she would never see him again, yet she was too young to speak about the subject of death. I found her very quiet and shy. Sometimes I had a feeling that she wanted to broach the subject but was hesitant. I also did not encourage her for I did not want to breakdown and make her miserable. On the morning of 29 December I went to her and wished her a very happy birthday and gave her a present. She did not look happy at all and said *"I would have a party if Bade Daddy was here."* I hugged her and replied, *"You are not having a party because your Mummy may be going to the hospital and give you a big present of a brother or sister. Why don't you invite a couple of friends who live close by for lunch and we can decorate the room also".* I saw the sparkle in her eyes come back which we all loved. I gave her a little money to go to the canteen which was nearby and get some balloons and bunting. I helped her to put up the balloons and realized that I had got back the Radhika as her grandfather knew her, full of life and fun, and she must also have found me more like the *Bari Ma* (grandmother) she had always known.

The next day Shyama had to go to the hospital. We left Radhika with some friends, and I went to the hospital with her. After a few hours in the ward she was shifted into the labour room and I was waiting patiently outside and praying for the welfare of both the mother and the child. Shyama had a normal delivery and when little Malavika was put in my arms, there ran in my veins a sort of happy current. God was kind: if he had taken away a precious life, He gave us another to love and look after. Shyama came home after a couple of days, her mother also arrived and I flew back to Chandigarh to be with my other granddaughter, Savita, who was left on her own for nearly two months staying with friends and relatives. Savita was naturally very happy to have her Nani back. I did not go out very much. I spent a lot of time teaching her Hindi, History and Civics. It was her first University exam and it gave me something to do and I quite enjoyed reading and reviving my knowledge of Hindi literature. Thus my grand-daughters were helping me to resume a normal life.

The next whiff of happiness came when Pavan returned home safely after a successful expedition to Antarctica. I went to Delhi to meet him because the whole team was being presented to the Prime Minister. I was staying with Indu and she mentioned to me that there was a gentleman from the Overseas Development Administration who was keen to marry her. On asking for more details she said *"He is actually posted in London and comes occasionally to check the work that is done here in India. I wish that you had met him when he came to the house to condole when Daddy died"*. I did remember that a British official had called with beautiful flowers. Indu received him, but I was too upset to meet a stranger and make polite conversation. I also remember very vividly what my husband said to me after Indu joined the British High Commission. *"I am sure that she will marry a foreigner"*, he said, *"It is only a question of time when she meets someone of her intellectual level"*. My answer was *"We only want her happiness. Let us see what destiny has in store for her. She deserves the best."*

I was highly appreciative of the gesture made by the gentleman, for Indu was quite new to the organization when N.P. died. As luck would have it, George Gwyer came to Delhi while I was still there. Indu invited him to the house. He struck me as a mature man, tall and strapping, forthright and pleasant. We spent about an hour together and I found myself quite comfortable with him. He was English, about 12 years senior to Indu, a divorcé who had three school-going sons. He was highly qualified, had a good job, and a pleasing personality. The whole situation gave me enough food for thought. Ultimately I came to the conclusion that I should allow Indu to make up her mind, and I would accept her decision.

In August 1984 we observed N.P.'s first *"Shradh"*, which is generally held sometime during the eleventh month after the death. It is a prayer or *"havan"*, and then some charity is done for the peace of the departed soul. Pavan was now in Dehra Dun so we all got together there. Praveen came from Lagos, and Indu from Delhi.

In October, a day before Diwali, we received the sad news of Deepak Vadhera's death (Nita's husband). My brother had lost two sons-in-law within two years, leaving young widows with school-going children bearing the loss. We were in the midst of the death prayers when we got the shocking news of Indira Gandhi's assassination. She was shot dead by two of her Sikh bodyguards. Hell was let loose in Delhi. Thousands of Sikhs were massacred, which left the community and the whole country stunned. After all, when Mahatma Gandhi was shot by a Maharashtrian the entire community was not attacked. Soon after, in early December 1984, the Bhopal gas leak tragedy occurred. Something went wrong in the Union Carbide factory and the gas leak caused the death of nearly twenty thousand people. Lakhs of people were affected with respiratory ailments and blindness, and even to this day there are people suffering, handicapped for life. Some compensation was given but too little, too late. It was one of the worst tragedies witnessed by industry. All these tragic happenings made me realize how fortunate I was to have the caring support of my husband for 42 years, and I was now determined that I think of him with love and affection, but not mourn for him.

Political Life 1967-1984

Shastriji's death came as a great shock to the nation. We had lost another honest, sincere patriot who had dedicated his life to the country. The question again arose, who was going to take over? It was an extremely difficult choice to make, till the high command of the Congress thought that instead of having a controversial figure at the top, it would be more convenient to have Indira Gandhi as the Prime Minister who would be like a puppet in their hands. She was inexperienced and docile, but being Nehru's daughter would be acceptable to everybody. The Congress President would be more powerful than the Prime Minister who would be a nominal head.

Indira had been hostess to her father ever since Independence. She was devoted to him and was living with her two sons in Teen Murti House. Her husband Feroze Gandhi, who was also in the Congress, was an extremely intelligent man. However, he chose not to live in his father-in-law's house, which put a strain on their marriage. Feroze died in 1960 and after Nehru's death in 1964, Indira was inducted into the Cabinet by Shastri as Minister of Information and Broadcasting. She had been the Congress President for a year in 1959. She was new to active politics, and did not do anything spectacular for a year or two, but by 1967 she was ready to assert herself, and there was a split in the Congress. The opposite side called itself the Congress O.

The people of India were very happy to have Indira as the Prime Minister, and when she was able to win the 14 day war against Pakistan, and a new state of Bangladesh was created, there was even more jubilation. In the 1971 elections, she was returned with an overwhelming majority. Her election was contested in court by Raj Narain stating that she had won by ignoring the electoral rules. Although the lapse was very minor, the Judge held that a law broken was enough reason for a person to be disqualified. Thus Indira should have resigned. That was the most honourable thing to do. In all probability she would have come in again with a thumping majority. But she chose to do nothing of that sort. She declared an Emergency, and promptly arrested Opposition members, and imposed press censorship. She did not seek anybody's advice, and when senior members like Jayprakash Narayan,

Morarji Desai and Bhim Sen Sachar advised her to withdraw the Emergency, she refused and put them in jail. The only person whom she trusted was her son Sanjay who became so powerful that it seemed that she was unable to control him. It is surprising to note that the masses were more upset with the state of affairs than the educated and the upper middle classes who did not raise their voice at all. In fact, there was a small group who even thought that the progress of the country would be quicker under a dictatorship rather than a democracy.

Indeed, she was now virtually a dictator, and the only voice that rose was of Jayprakash Narayan who was in favour of total revolution and appealed to the youth to stand up for their rights. Alas he was too ill, and was arrested and languished in jail. All the Chief Ministers of the States were taking orders from Sanjay and obeying them. One order was the sterilisation programme, and the other was the cleaning up of the slum areas, without providing alternative accommodation. In 1977, Indira was so sure of winning that she withdrew the Emergency and ordered the sixth General Election. This time she was in for a shock. She and Sanjay both lost their seats, and the Congress was ousted. Everybody was happy that there would now be a new Government which would be progressive and people were all looking forward to a coalition of Janta Dal and Samaj Wadi parties. Morarji Desai, Jagjivan Ram and Charan Singh were the three main persons. Very soon people realized that there was internal bickering for the top office, till Jayprakash advised them that Morarji should be chosen. The others agreed reluctantly, but were unhappy with the decision.

All that the Morarji Government did was to appoint a Commission under a retired judge of the Supreme Court, Justice Shah, to go in to the irregularities committed by the previous Government. Indira Gandhi was put under house arrest. The Governor of Delhi during the Emergency was Kishan Chand, a personal friend of ours. He was supposed to testify before the Shah Commission but was found dead, drowned in a well. We felt very sorry about Kishan Chand's death. It was a sad end to a brilliant career.

The public was sadly disappointed with the Janata Government and when Charan Singh withdrew his support, fresh elections were ordered in 1980. This time Indira's Congress (I) came back again with a clear majority. Her slogan of *Garibi Hatao* [66] caught the imagination of the public; forgotten were the irregularities of the Emergency.

Over the years, the States had become a little tired of the dictates of the Centre, and several parties came up in different States with only the welfare of their State at heart. Thus the Dravida Munnetra Kazhigam (DMK) became powerful in Tamil Nadu, the Akali Dal (a Sikh organization) in Punjab, the Janta and the Samajvadi party in Uttar Pradesh, and the Communist Party of India (Marxist) in Bengal.

By this time I was sad and disappointed by the return of Indira and I lost faith in politics. To my mind the stalwarts who had sacrificed their lives to win Independence had all gone. The present day politicians were mostly people who wanted to take up politics as self seekers rather than patriots, who worked more for personal gain and less for serving the country. People with criminal cases against them were contesting elections. Decent educated people wanted to stay away from politics thinking that it was a dirty game. In the Rajya Sabha there were some intellectuals, but their voice really did not carry much weight.

Soon after Indira returned, Sanjay who was arrogant, aggressive and rash, lost control of an aircraft, crashed and lay dead on the ground. He left behind his young widow, Maneka, a Punjabi Sikh girl, and a toddler son Varun. His death came as a great shock to the country, and I can well imagine how it must have affected his mother, but she put up a brave face, and insisted that her elder son Rajiv should give up his job. He was a pilot with Indian Airlines, married to an Italian girl, Sonia, with two young children, Rahul and Priyanka. Rajiv fought the by-election for the seat that fell vacant on Sanjay's death. Maneka had thought that after her husband's death she would occupy his shoes and take his place. Indira did not permit this. She made Rajiv her assistant. Sonia Gandhi had never been in favour of her husband joining politics but destiny was too strong and she had to give in to the wishes of her mother-in-law. Thus politics was more or less inflicted on him. Rajiv was an educated young man who had all the qualities of a gentleman. The relationship between Maneka and her mother-in-law soured day by day, and Maneka fell out of favour. She also proved to be a strong woman, joined the Opposition and became a Member of Parliament, and has opposed her husband's family ever since.

During this time several parties had come into existence and the Congress had lost its majority in many States. The Akalis [67] in the Punjab were able to defeat the Congress. Indira in turn encouraged a Sikh Jathedar [68] of the Golden Temple of Amritsar to be even more staunch a Sikh, and helped him financially to gain more power. When he became really powerful he started thinking of an independent Sikh state called Khalistan. He thought that if the Muslims could get an Independent Pakistan on the strength of their religion, why not the Sikhs?

Terrorism came to the fore. Sikhs who had shed their beards and long hair also become targets, and the Hindus started feeling insecure. The Golden Temple, instead of being a place of worship, became an armoury. Indira now had to take decisive action.

While in Chandigarh I could sense that there were lots of Sikhs who respected Jarnail Singh Bhindranwale. There were, of course, the more moderates who did not agree with the concept of Khalistan, but were reluctant to express their views for fear of a backlash from their own community. Indira now ordered the army to walk into the Golden Temple and clear it of all the followers of Bhindranwale. It was an irony of fate that Zail Singh, who was a Sikh and the President of India, signed the order. The troops that went into the temple were also led by a Sikh. Bhindranwale was killed with his followers, but several innocent Sikhs who had gone to the temple for prayers were also killed. The temple itself, the highest seat of the Sikh religion, was badly damaged. The Sikh community was very hurt. The community as a whole did not want to be separated, they are very much part and parcel of the country and have always shown their patriotism. Their valiant role in the armed forces is well known.

Indira thought she had achieved a great victory, but she had to pay for it with her own life. In October 1984, she was shot dead by two of her Sikh bodyguards, who never forgave her for soiling the sanctity of the Golden Temple. But the Sikh community had to pay a heavy price. During the next 48 hours, thousands of Sikh men, women, and children were killed, their property looted and burned.

A similar communal incident occurred in Gujarat in 2002, when thousands of Muslims were killed as a reaction to the Godhra train fire in which many Hindus were burned to death while returning from doing *Kar Seva* [69] at the Babri Masjid site in Ayodhya. Such events bring to mind the trauma of Partition, and the need for us as a nation to avoid any sparks that can fuel communal tensions.

Indu's Marriage and My Trip to Khartoum

I was now back in Chandigarh with Praveen. On 26 January 1985, Republic Day, Pavan was awarded the Vishisht Seva Medal (VSM) for his distinguished service on his trip to Antarctica. I was naturally very happy and had a lovely thanksgiving prayer in the house and gave the guests a lavish coffee party. This was the first time I entertained after N.P.'s death.

In March I went to Agra to see Madhu who had fractured his leg in a train accident. This time Indu told me she had made up her mind to marry George who had switched to the European Community as it was known then (now it is called the European Union), and was posted in Khartoum, Sudan. I was very happy with her decision and tried to make enquiries as to how the marriage was to take place, since it was an international and inter-religious marriage. We were told that a Hindu marriage could not take place when one of the partners was a Christian. The only alternative was a court marriage. A month's notice had to be put up in court. So George came on 14 May 1985, and a notice was put up that Indu and George wanted to marry. The earliest the wedding could be held was 14 June, now that the preliminaries had been worked out, so 14 June 1985 was fixed for the marriage. On 14 May we announced Indu's engagement and had a small family get together in the evening with music and dancing and dinner. George left the next morning for Sudan, and said that he would be back on 14 June which was a Friday, spend a couple of days with us, and return to Khartoum on the Sunday. Indu was not inclined to give up her job till she was married and said she would do so after the ceremony. That meant that they would have a delayed honeymoon. George arrived very much in time and they were officially married in the morning. In the evening we had the Hindu ceremony of *Jai Mala* [70] at Tara's house (where Indu had been staying for the last two years) but the actual Hindu ceremony was not performed.

Instead we had a small religious ceremony seeking blessings from God followed by a vegetarian meal with all the relations. Pavan, Shyama and the children were there and so was Praveen. On Saturday I had thrown a cocktail party at the British High

Major Pavan Nair receiving the
Vishisht Seva Medal from
Army Chief General Arun Vaidya,
1986

MALAVIKA, SHYAMA, PAVAN, BASANT
AND RADHIKA IN PUNE, 1996

GEORGE, INDU AND MARCUS WITH
BASANT IN PUNE, 1996

Commission hall where all our friends and relations were invited, as well as some of Indu's friends from the British High Commission. It was a lovely evening, everybody was happy to meet the newly weds and more so because they knew the marriage had taken place with my knowledge, consent and blessings. On Sunday morning George and Indu went to Agra for the day and late at night George flew back to England and Sudan. Indu followed him after six weeks and came to see me in December when I threw a party for the Chandigarh friends at the Thursday Club.

Both George and Indu came again in August 1986 and stayed with us for a couple of weeks in Dehra Dun. It was a pleasure to have them with us. Pavan and Shyama took them to Mussoorie, and then we had a trip to Hardwar where George thoroughly enjoyed his dip in the Ganges. He liked Indian food and we all felt very comfortable and at home with each other. It is always very gratifying for parents to see their children well settled and happy. It gave me great pleasure to know that George and Indu had brought a flat in Hove, and when I saw some of the photos I could well visualize the flat and realize what a good choice they had made. George was very keen that I should visit them in Khartoum for a holiday, and since I was not doing anything in India I accepted the invitation. After a gap of several years, my travels started once again.

Indu and George had a spacious, double-storied house, well-furnished, and the garden was reasonably good. Sudan has very little rainfall in the north where it is more a dry desert place. Care had been taken to put plants that needed very little water. A lot of stress was put on bougainvilleas, as they bloom during the summer and do not need much water, while adding a lot of colour to the garden.

There were a few Indian families living in the neighbourhood and what I liked about George was that he was quite happy meeting them and being friendly. There were also his own colleagues who were from France, the Netherlands and Denmark. They were fluent in English so we were able to converse with them also. We came to know that there was a big Gujarati community in Omdurman and they celebrated the *Navratras* in a big way. We went there to attend the function, and I was surprised to see the scale on which they were celebrating. There was plenty of food and soft drinks. Ladies were dressed in their finest outfits, dancing and singing to Indian music, particularly the *Garba* dance with sticks which is special to Gujarat. I had never attended a function like this anywhere, even in India.

Navratras are celebrated in Punjab also, where the first eight days are dedicated to *Mata*, the Mother goddess. This is also the time when almost all villages and towns enact the Ramayana, which is called *Ram Lila*, a cultural programme of the story of Shri Ram who killed Ravana, a demon god who had abducted Sita, Shri Ram's wife. On the 10th day that is called Dussehra, the effigies of Ravana, his brother Kumbh Karan and son Megh Nath are burnt in an open ground, where a big fair is held. There are fireworks and an atmosphere of joy and victory prevail. It is really considered the victory of good over evil. In Bengal the same ten days are dedicated to the Goddess Durga and her children Lakshmi, the Goddess of wealth, Saraswati, the Goddess of learning, and her two sons, Ganesh, with the head of an elephant, is the God of wisdom, and Kartik, the God of pomp and splendour. These ten days are considered very auspicious all over India, although they are celebrated a little differently in different regions.

The Indian community in Sudan was very friendly and when I saw puries I asked from where they obtained the wheat flour *atta*. They very willingly told us that an Indian lady was selling the special Indian spices and dals. So I got some *atta* and *besan* gram flour and lots of Punjabi food was introduced in the household.

When I made *pakoras* [71] they were a great success in all the cocktail parties that were held by George and Indu. During my stay, George's sons visited from England and thoroughly enjoyed their vacation. It was good to see them enjoying Indian food.

George and Indu loved going out for long drives. I particularly remember one on a Sunday morning when we went to see the place where the Blue Nile and the White Nile meet. It was very fascinating to see a clear demarcation in the colours of the water, on one side it was blue, on the other side white. The return journey became quite an experience. George decided to take a different route and we soon found ourselves in a sandy area, and the car started giving trouble. It stopped and refused to move. George had to push it and it moved. After a little while it stopped again. Fortunately we were near a small hamlet with 2 or 3 hutments. The men there helped us again and also gave us a little water to drink which was very welcome. I could well understand the plight of these poor people who were living in such difficult surroundings of sand storms, heat and dust, with scarcity of water. It was very uncomfortable because it was in the middle of the afternoon when the sun was very strong. I was very concerned about George who had to stand in that heat and push the car. I dare say that he must have also been quite worried, but he tried to make little of it. Needless to say, we were very relieved when we got the sight of a proper road. It was a very novel and exciting experience. It gave me insight into the life of people who travel in the deserts and what they have to experience.

I was very impressed to see one of Mother Teresa's homes in Khartoum, and one day, Indu, George and I paid a visit. I was very surprised to find Indian nuns in sarees with blue borders attending to the very old and little babies. I was told that none of the nuns understood Arabic at all, and of the three or four Indian women only one could speak English. She was able to explain to the others what was required of them. It was an eye-opener to see so much dedication and we were highly appreciative of the excellent work they were doing.

Since Khartoum was considered a hardship posting, once a year the officials got a week off for rest and recuperation. This notion was quite new to me, but I could well understand that Europeans who had to work in these hard conditions deserved a little extra rest. George and Indu decided on a holiday to Mombasa and Nairobi. This meant further sightseeing for me. We had a most enjoyable holiday in Mombasa where we stayed in a beautiful hotel by the seaside and spent delightful mornings on the beach. George did windsurfing also, but

Indu joined him only for swimming. This was perhaps the only time that I regretted not having made an effort to learn swimming. I could easily have learnt when my children were learning, but I suppose I was too lazy. In the evenings we would go to different restaurants and enjoy the ambience created by different architects, and also enjoy different cuisine. Africa is famous for its safari outings. George was quite keen to go for a couple of nights, but both Indu and I were a little reluctant. I have never been fond of animals and the wild animals gave me a feeling of a little lurking fear. So it was decided that we would visit a wild animal sanctuary which was not very far for a day trip. I was quite happy with this arrangement for I felt that my education of Africa would be quite incomplete if I did not avail of this opportunity. So we went in the afternoon and were driving through the sanctuary when there was a sudden cloudburst and there was torrential rain. Suddenly it was very dark and George had to switch on the headlights to be able to move at a snail's speed. Once the lights were on we could see the wild animals which also seemed panic stricken running all over the place. With great difficulty George was able to find his way and we heaved a sigh of relief when we were out of the game park. If the sand dunes and heat were bad, this was worse, but both were memorable experiences.

The two days in Nairobi were delightful. We were staying in a beautiful hotel. Flowers adorned the room and fresh fruit, nuts and chocolates lay in the fridge. The food served was of excellent quality and finely garnished. In short, this was my most enjoyable holiday and exciting week so far. I then did not know that many more holidays were in store for me with Indu and George, and if someone asked me to choose the best holiday, I would be in a quandary, each one was better than the other.

On our return from Kenya, we received intimation that my sister-in-law Kuntibibi had passed away. I was very close to her and felt the loss, but since I was so far away it was not possible for me to return to Delhi immediately. Even telephones were difficult and I was able to get in touch through the radio, which was far from satisfactory. Just as I was planning my return to Delhi, Indu realized that she may be pregnant, so I postponed my departure till her pregnancy was confirmed by the doctors. We were all very happy with the news. Indu was keen that I should stay on and go to England with her where the child would be born. I felt a little differently. I had planned a holiday of three months and this would mean well over a year. George then gave a good suggestion; that I should return to Delhi for a couple of months and rejoin Indu who would have to go to England at least three months before the baby was due. Pavan was now posted in Delhi so I returned to Delhi and spent some time with Brother and Pavan. I now decided to give up my cottage in Chandigarh as I had not used it for over two years. I was sure that I could make my home with Pavan and Shyama.

An Interlude in England

I returned to Khartoum in May 1987, a week before George and Indu were due to leave for England. On our way we spent a couple of days in Amsterdam. This was my first visit to Europe. We had two very hectic days in Amsterdam. Besides visiting the wonderful museum of Van Gogh, there were other art galleries and diamond factories, and boat rides along the canals during the evenings. We even went to The Hague and the International Court of Justice, and Delft, famous for pottery.

We stayed in the Americana, a five star hotel, and when I saw the menu and the exorbitant prices my hunger would have died a natural death, but George was careful to let me order the chicken before he handed me the menu card!

We reached Sussex, and first went to George's mother's house in Ovingdean for a cup of tea where I had the pleasure of meeting Mrs Gwyer senior and George's sister Brenda. They were living in a comfortable bungalow with a pretty garden and fine views of the sea, on the other side of Brighton, about 5 km from Hove. We spent the night in a hotel close to the flat and next morning while Indu and I took time getting ready and having breakfast, George went off and we followed him after a while. When we reached we found George had already opened up lots of things and the kitchen was set.

I was delighted to see Indu's flat, which was part of a converted mansion. Marlborough Court, a listed building, had been the home of the Duchess of Marlborough in the 1880s. Her grand-nephew, Winston Churchill, used to visit her when he was at school nearby in Hove. It was well situated, the sea was in front and on the side was a lovely garden, with a shopping area at the back which involved a walk of about 5 minutes. It had a large kitchen and a very spacious drawing room. The flat was semi-furnished, and they needed a sofa set for their drawing room. Next day we went to a department store, Hannington's in Brighton, and saw a Wordsworth sofa set which we liked very much. It was not ultra modern, but was not old fashioned either. The decision was made, and an expensive item was bought in less than ten minutes. Any other man might have spent much more time

INDIAN SPRING

in choosing a tie. I realized that George was quick in making up his mind and then never chose to regret his decision. Once we were settled nicely, George went back to Khartoum and came back on his annual leave a week before Marcus was due to arrive. A day or two after his arrival, England witnessed one of its worst hurricanes, storms or cyclones. Whatever it was, it was terrible. It occurred late at night, with a strong wind blowing, rain lashing the windows, thunder and lightning, and the sound of the roaring sea, quite frightening! I could hear George and Indu moving about, trying to find a place far away from the windows. I stayed in bed. I did have a little experience of thunderstorms and cyclonic weather, because the winds from the Bay of Bengal used to play havoc and often some of the villages of East Bengal were inundated with water and floods. In Calcutta it usually meant uprooted trees, a break down of electricity supplies and telephone lines, and blocked roads. I lay in bed and only prayed that Indu should not start her labour pains. It would be impossible to take her to the hospital under such terrible conditions. At last the rain and wind subsided. In the morning I realized that the devastation was on a scale similar to India's. But the difference became obvious when within a few hours the electricity and telephone lines were restored. The roads were cleared. In India it would have taken days to deal with such a calamity. I tried to find excuses for India, it was after all a vast country, but then we have vast resources too. What India lacks is determination, we only want the Government to do everything for us. As citizens we can only think of donating a little money. It is gratifying to note that now quite a few Non Governmental Organisations (NGOs) have come up which do excellent work. Within a week of the storm a campaign for planting more trees had started. The uprooted trees had to be replaced with fresh saplings, so that within a few years the landscape would be the same if not better. What struck me most was that this was a voluntary effort.

On Sunday 25 October 1987 George went to church in the morning. I found Indu very depressed, because the child was overdue by about six days. I suggested to her that to relieve her of her worry we would go to the hospital for a check up. When George returned I told him that before planning the programme for the day, we must visit the hospital to put Indu's mind at rest. So it was decided that after the visit to the hospital we would go out to an Italian restaurant for lunch. On reaching the hospital, the nurse attached a machine to Indu which would indicate the condition of the child. This would take about 45 minutes. The first 40 minutes went off peacefully and then suddenly the machine started making a terrible noise. I thought that something had gone wrong with the electricity. The nurse rushed to fetch the doctor who immediately said *"The child is in distress and must be taken out"*. Before we knew what was happening, Indu was wheeled into the operation theatre and within fifteen minutes the nurse came out smiling and said that a son was born and both mother and child were alright.

The fifteen minutes that George and I spent were absolute agony. The news came as a great relief; the feeling of joy came later. Before we met Indu, we saw the baby. George had to rush home to get the packed suitcase which had Indu's and baby's clothes. By the time we returned Indu had been brought to the ward and we saw little Marcus, thin but tall weighing 8 pounds. How strong was Indu's premonition that she needed attention, how fortunate it was that the machine gave an indication after forty minutes. If another five minutes had gone by, we would have just thought that Indu was worrying unnecessarily. Everything was alright and we were all very happy. Granny Gwyer and Aunty Brenda came to the hospital in the evening. It was a pleasure to see the joy writ on their faces. After a few weeks, just before George returned to Khartoum, we had a lovely get-together of the whole Gwyer family. George's brother, Richard, and his wife Sydney, were there with their children. George's Aunt

Freda (Mrs Gwyer's sister), and her family were also there to celebrate. It was pleasing to see such a close knit family. Marcus' elder brothers were delighted to see the baby. I felt perfectly at home with all members of the family, and realized that family ties are strong all over the world and not just restricted to India.

Marcus was a good, smiley baby. We had to wait till he was six weeks old before we could leave England. George left when his leave expired. We faced the English winter and were glad to get back to Khartoum where there was more sunshine.

Praveen and R.K. Return from Lagos

While I was still in England I came to know that Pavan was allotted a flat in Pune for which he had applied through the Army Welfare scheme. I was delighted for I was very keen that he should have his own flat and Shyama had chosen Pune for she felt that it was an educational centre and Pavan was a Bombay Sapper and knew Pune very well. With the temperate climate they could settle down in Pune after retiring.

I returned from Sudan in January 1987, and R.K. and Praveen came from Nigeria to India for a month's holiday. I felt that R.K. was now keen to return to India. I also encouraged them because Savita was about 21 and of marriageable age. They returned in February 1989, and we were all together in Pavan's house in the Cantonment. R.K. and Praveen were on the look out for suitable accommodation which they could buy and then settle down permanently in Delhi. During their stay Pavan and Shyama went for a holiday to England and America and I also went to England for a couple of months as Indu was there by herself with Marcus. Mrs Kher, Shyama's mother also came to Delhi to be with the children while their parents were away.

It took R.K. and Praveen a while to find a suitable flat in Noida. Sector 15 was just coming up and the flat was not even fully ready for occupation, but they shifted when the contractors were able to hand them the keys. On my return from England I found them nicely settled in this three bedroom flat which had been done up beautifully. Like R.K., Praveen always had an artistic eye and whatever they had in the flat was tasteful and made the flat very attractive. Savita was selected for a course in fashion designing and joined the National Institute of Fashion Technology (NIFT). Prashant got a seat in the APS school which was just about a kilometre away from their flat. R.K. was back to work, and it was good to see them settle so well in Noida. It has been a source of great joy to me that all three of my children have their own properties, and are all enjoying living in them.

Taiji Passes Away

In early 1990, Pavan was posted to Chandi Mandir near Chandigarh to command his Regiment with the rank of full Colonel. He had not been allotted accommodation and we were still in Delhi. The plan was that once the children finished their exams, Shyama and the girls would join Pavan and stay in the mess for a while, and I would go to Mount Abu and join the family when Pavan got a proper house. We had to give up the house in Delhi once the children's exams were over, which was the end of April.

In Delhi I was in the habit of ringing up Chandji (whom the children always addressed as Taiji) at least once a week to find out how she was and if she needed anything. We would visit her once every three or four weeks. We were supposed to leave Delhi in a week and were in the midst of packing when I rang her up and got no reply. I tried again after an hour but again there was no answer. In the evening when I rang up again and the ring was quite normal and still there was no response, I felt very worried and panicky. I asked Sheila who was in Delhi if she could arrange to send someone to Chandji's house to see what was the matter. She rang me up within a few minutes to say that Chandji had picked up the phone and spoken in a very feeble voice that she was not well. On receiving this news, Shyama and I decided to go to Old Delhi immediately. I carried a small bag with a couple of changes, in case I had to spend the night there. We found her in a very bad shape. She had fever and was breathing with a lot of difficulty. It appeared that the house had been unattended, and so had she, during the previous three days, which meant that she could not have had much nourishment either. I was rather disappointed that the neighbours had never bothered to see her or inform us of her illness. We had left our telephone number with them in case of need. Chandji needed attention and care. Shyama was not willing to leave me with her. So Shyama just decided to bring her home.

The next morning the doctor was called in. With intensive medicines and care, Chandji showed marked improvement within forty eight hours. It was obvious that she needed looking after and it was equally clear that we had to vacate the house within a week. So I asked all my nieces and nephews from the Nair side to come and meet me at 11 am the next day as I had some urgent work with them. They all came and I told them that Taiji needed to be looked after for at least a month. By that time Pavan would be able to get a house and then she would be shifted to Chandigarh. All of them were ready to undertake the task, but I felt that she would be most comfortable with Sheila, whose husband was Director of the Central Bureau of Investigation (CBI) and had a spacious bungalow in New Delhi.

Pavan rented a private four bedroom bungalow in Panchkula and exactly after a month he went to Delhi and brought Chandji with him to Chandigarh. I also returned from Mount Abu. She was now looked after and cared for by Pavan and Shyama and of course I was there to keep her company and help see to her needs. A full time maid was engaged to look after her. She was extremely weak and would hardly get out of bed for fifteen minutes to sit out on the verandah. She was not in acute pain but was just getting weaker day by day and slowly withering away. She died after a fifteen months' stay with us. Unfortunately I was not there as I was away to England for six weeks to be with Indu who was alone in England.

Thus passed away a good God-fearing woman, who really bore her long illness without complaining, most patiently awaited her end. She was denied motherhood but was given a most dignified farewell by Pavan and Shyama, better than any son could have given. I was told about the chanting of the Vedic mantras and the learned Brahmins who conducted the 13th day prayer for the peace of her soul. All this was done because Pavan knew her views of being an orthodox Hindu who would have wanted the traditional way, as was observed when her husband died. She was able to live on her own for several years because she was extremely frugal and never wasted any money. Besides that, the rent she paid for the house, which had been rented by her brother in the Shri Ram Institute in 1947, was very nominal. Much later, when the rents were sky high, the Institute did take her to Court and wanted the house vacated. Fortunately for her, the Court took a very sympathetic attitude. In view of her age, delicate health, and being a childless widow, she was allowed to continue living in that house, without raising the rent, till her death. She left wedding gifts for Radhika and Malavika, and the rest of the money was to be given in charity, particularly for the upliftment of girls and women in distress. In fact when Shyama started the NGO *Asha* in Pune, part of Taiji's money was the first donation.

N.P.'s Two Sisters

I have written at length about Dewan Sahib, Rajaji, and Chandji because they were with us and all three passed away under our care. There was a lot of interaction with K.P. also. To complete the Nair family history, I will now write about N.P.'s two sisters.

When I got married, Kaushalya Behanji[72] had given birth to her 8th child, and after that three more arrived who were more or less the same age as my children. I met her for the first time in 1944 when I attended her eldest daughter Kanta's marriage in Lahore, and spent a couple of days with her while she was extremely busy. I really had an opportunity to see her at close quarters when I spent about six months with Dewan Sahib in Ambala in 1957. Sodhi Sahib was also posted there; he had built a house next to ours. The three elder girls were married and so was the eldest son. The second son Jagdish had joined the Air Force, while two of her sons were under training at the Joint Services Wing (JSW) and Indian Military Academy (IMA) in Pune and Dehra Dun. She ran a simple home, served wholesome food to the children, and gave an impression of being a very kind and patient woman who was very loving to her children. Her husband, Jijaji, was more for discipline and saw that the children tended the garden, did various household chores, and they were always well turned out. They attended local schools, and their results were always good.

Ajit and Kiran were of the same age as Pavan and Praveen, so they had a lovely time together. As Ajit and Kiran had to go to school, it meant that my children were also able to put in a couple of hours with the tutors I hired for them. They enjoyed their stay in Ambala, and did not miss their friends of Kanpur.

This also gave me an opportunity to meet Santosh who spent about three months in Ambala with her parents and gave birth to a baby girl. I did not meet Bimla, who was married to an Army officer until he retired from service and they shifted into their own house in Chandigarh. Soon after her husband passed away and she has now moved to Noida and lives in her own Army flat which was allotted to her a few years ago.

While I was still there, Jagdish was reported missing on a flight somewhere in Kashmir. To this day, the debris of the plane has not been located. As usual, several surmises and theories were afloat. He may by mistake have entered into Pakistan (and been taken prisoner) or even into Russia. Astrologers were consulted who advocated different pujas and gave hope. However, he was presumed dead when nothing was found after several aerial searches which yielded no clue. I got a glimpse of Kaushalya Behanji's strong character when, within a month of Jagdish's death, the third son Mohini was to become an officer in the Indian Army and the passing out parade was to be held in Dehra Dun. She decided to attend the parade. *"I cannot allow my loss to mar the achievement of my son who is becoming an officer. It is a great day for him and I must be there to share his joy."*

Inder and Ashok also joined the army, but Vinod was keen to go to America, and Behanji encouraged him to go. He made a grand success of his career, helped other brothers and sisters and their children to visit America, and assisted them in their studies and jobs. Over the years Jijaji and Behanji also visited him. Vinod married a lady doctor from south India, and she became successful in her own right. Later on, Jijaji met with an accident, and both Behanji and Jijaji spent their time with the three sons who were in the Army, according to where they were posted. Jijaji died before N.P., but Behanji passed away in December 1991 in Delhi at the age of nearly 82. I was in Delhi at the time and was able to pay my last respects to her. I was now the only person alive out of the five brothers and sisters and their spouses.

Prakash Behanji's story is a bit different. She was also married and had three children when I came on the scene. Jijaji (Prakash Chand) came from a rich prosperous family, was handsome, and qualified as a lawyer. But he was not able to set up a practice and chose to go to England and find a career there. He went with the family, and came back without finding anything suitable there. When I got married he was working with Tatas, and in 1947 he was posted to Lahore, and subsequently had to come out. He then got a job in Lucknow which enabled them to rehabilitate themselves.

Inder[73] joined the Air Force and then shifted to Hindustan Aeronautics Ltd in Bangalore. Chander was also working. Jijaji went back to Tatas and continued with them until he retired. Sheila obtained an MA from Delhi University, and married Raju. After being in Delhi until 1960, Jijaji and Behanji made their home with Inder and Reena in Bangalore and lived with them to the end. From Bangalore they used to come to the north every three or four years to spend a little time with Sheila, and they also came to us for a month or two. It was a pleasure to have them with us. They had certain admirable qualities. They were always at peace, with no complaints, quite content with their simple lives. Jijaji had seen real luxurious life, but never seemed to miss it. He was happy that he had good children and were looked after by Inder and Reena to the best of their ability. They had charming manners and when they had to be hospitalized in Bangalore, the doctors and nurses were so taken with their polite ways, that they received very good treatment in return.

Jijaji died first, Behanji after a gap of five or six years. During this time she came to us twice and spent time with us. She always had a good word to say about her children and their spouses, particularly Reena who really looked after them. Since they both died in Bangalore we were not able to be present for their funerals. Much later I had occasion of meeting Inder and Reena when they decided to shift to Pune after Inder retired from service. They settled in Pune, very close to Pavan's flat in Salunke Vihar. Sadly, Inder Varma passed away on 18 January 2005 after a long illness borne patiently. We shall remember him as a fine man with very gentle ways.

This more or less concludes the story of the Nair family. All I can say is that I receive a lot of love and affection from all the nephews and nieces and their spouses whenever I meet them. I have had close contact with Brigadier Inder Sodhi and his wife Pramila who have also settled in Pune, and it gives me great pleasure to have my nephews and their families around me.

The Wedding Season

Coming back to my own life, I returned from England about a month after Chandji's death in 1991. Indu and George also came for a few days, on their way to Solomon Islands where George had been appointed Head of Delegation of the European Commission. The conditions in Chandigarh were a little disturbed so George could not come to Chandigarh. Indu came for a few days and then both of us went to Delhi to spend a little time with R.K. and Praveen. Just as Indu left, I found myself in the midst of a wedding season. As most of my nephews and nieces were born in the 1930s and 1940s, they had mostly got married in the 1950s and 1960s. Now the next generation was ready to settle down.

The first on the list was Piyush, grandson of Nirmala and son of Madhu and Milan. He was only twenty two, but had joined his father's business. He had chosen his life partner in Punita, daughter of a good friend of his parents. The families had known each other for years and were the disciples of Shri Maharajji[74] and had occasion to spend time together in Mount Abu. Punita was just about seventeen, and both of them decided, instead of approaching their parents, to go straight to Maharajji seeking his consent and blessings. Maharajji did not disappoint them but suggested that they should wait for at least one year to be sure that they wanted the union. Thus their engagement took place in December 1991, and they were married in January 1992. It was a grand affair because it meant celebrations in Agra and Delhi. Madhu and Milan have a very lavish life style, every detail had been thought out very carefully, and it was a most enjoyable wedding.

Before Piyush got married, there was another wedding. Brother's grand-daughter Shalini, Arjun and Amrita's daughter, got married to a young man from Puerto Rico whom she met in the USA while studying for her PhD. Carlos was her class mate and the wedding took place in Delhi. The Hindu marriage was performed in the presence of the immediate family. The following day, a lovely lunch was laid for friends and relations. It was a bright, sunny, Sunday afternoon, and we were all very happy to meet Carlos, who has a very pleasing personality.

It was now the turn of Sarlabibi's grandson, Rajen and Gieta's son, Mano Viraj. Although Rajen was posted in Calcutta, they decided to have the wedding in Delhi, as both Rajen and Gieta's parents could not undertake the journey to Calcutta. This was another big affair with lots of family get-togethers, dancing and music, with religious *Kirtans*[75] also. The girl's people's hospitality was on the same scale, and the reception after the wedding thrown by Gieta's parents at their farm in Chattarpur was very lavish.

On enquiring about the young bride, I was told that Viraj had known her for several years and had decided to marry when he was properly settled. So the trend of choosing one's own life partner which was set by Pavan and Indu, was now becoming almost a set pattern, for even Kay's daughter Namrita had also chosen her own life partner (Mihir) and so did her brother Gaurav much later. Fortunately, all of them had made very good choices and the parents had no reason to object.

This does not mean that arranged marriages were out. By and large, they were still very much accepted by society. Gautam, Kay and G.P.'s eldest son, married Manisha and they live in New York. This was an arranged marriage. Savita's marriage was another example of this traditional way. A niece of Kuntibibi had met Savita and recommended Janardhan, a young

Khatri boy who was in the merchant navy, as a suitable match for her. Brother referred the matter to Praveen and asked her to follow up. The young man's parents lived in Delhi, after retiring from the tea estates. Janardhan was at sea, and the parents were keen to find a bride for him, so that when he returned they would be able to recommend a suitable girl. Praveen and Kay went to see them and were highly impressed. Praveen and R.K. then invited them. They came to meet Savita and R.K., and were very happy to meet the family. Once Janardhan returned, they got in touch with R.K. and a further meeting was arranged. Both the girl and the young man were very impressed with each other, and after three or four meetings, they took the vital decision. Janardhan had returned in the middle of January, and on 1 February 1992, which was also his birthday, the engagement took place. The wedding was fixed for 6 March.

Thus after attending three marriages, I became busy with the preparations for Savita's wedding. While Praveen busied herself with getting the trousseau ready, R.K. and I got down to making all the arrangements. R.K. took a lot of trouble designing the wedding invitation with a beautiful Ganeshji on the top cover. The marriage ceremony took place in Noida with only the families present. The formal dinner was held at the Gymkhana Club, with family and friends and it all went off very well. We had a ladies' *sangeet* [76] a day before the wedding. The Kapurs held a delightful dinner *sangeet* a couple of days before the wedding, and held a dinner reception a day after the wedding. I was not able to attend this function as Praveen suddenly felt unwell. R.K. went and so did his sisters and gave us a glowing report of the function.

By the grace of God, this marriage has also worked out very successfully. Over the years, Savita and Janardhan have bought a beautiful flat and they are parents of a very lovely and lively son, Aryaman.

Pavan, Shyama and their children came for the wedding, but only for a day. Pavan was on an exercise and could not take much leave. Radhika was in the middle of her exams, so Shyama also had to return a day after the wedding. It was good that they were able to make it, for the *Mama Mami* [77] have a very important role of putting the *Chura* [78], which are a sign of the newly-weds. Indu was not able to attend the wedding because she had gone to Solomon Islands before there was any inkling that the wedding would take place.

SAVITA'S ENGAGEMENT, DELHI, 1992

FRONT ROW (LEFT TO RIGHT): SAVITA, JANARDHAN, PRASHANT

BACK ROW: PREM KAPUR, RAMI KAPUR, BASANT, PRAVEEN, RAJINDER

The Marriage of Savita and Janardhan, Delhi, 1992

PRAVEEN AND RAJINDER, 2004

MARCUS AND PRASHANT, 1994

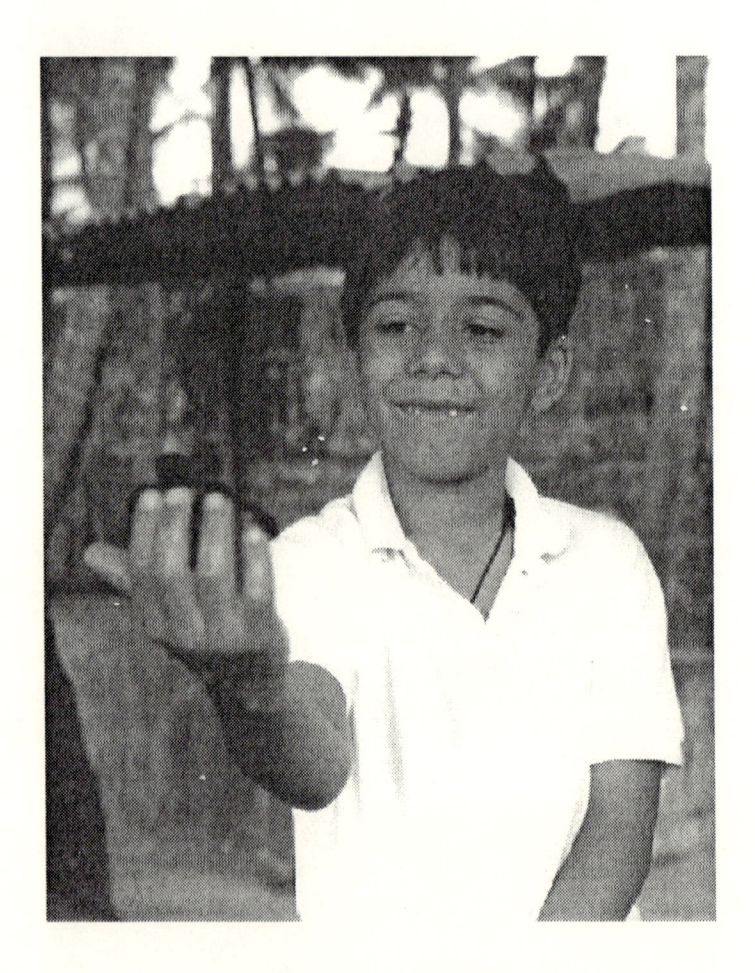

ARYAMAN, 2003

I had promised Indu that I would visit her in Solomon Islands and decided to make a trip straight from Delhi. I had been in Delhi right from October 1991 to March 1992. It gave me a lot of time with R.K. and Praveen, and also with Brother at the farm.

Visit to Solomon Islands

When Indu had gone to the Solomons, she flew straight to Singapore, spent a night in a hotel, and then flew on to Brisbane and Honiara. I did not want to spend a night in a hotel anywhere, and asked Arjun and G.P. to arrange my ticketing in such a way that I would spend the night in the air. G.P. was able to get the ticketing done, but it involved two nights in the aircraft, and three changes instead of two. I had never travelled such a long distance alone. On previous trips it was always with George and Indu. I never had to bother about my luggage and even my hand baggage was carried by them. All I had to do was to carry my purse and the boarding card, which was only handed to me the moment before I had to surrender it. The only care that I had to take was to see that my saree did not get stuck in the escalator. I was naturally a bit excited, the journey started late at night with Air France to Bangkok, a halt of six hours there, and then a short hop with Singapore Airlines to arrive in

Singapore in the afternoon. There I spent nearly eight hours before I continued to Brisbane, arriving there at 6.30 am after a flight of seven hours. From there it was only a flight of three hours to Honiara, the capital of Solomon Islands.

I think Arjun and Indu were more apprehensive about my travelling alone than I was. Arjun very sweetly took me out for a last minute shopping and suggested, *"We are so close to our doctor, why don't you get your blood pressure checked?"* I readily agreed, but when we got to the doctor he said, *"Now that we are here, why not get an electro-cardiogram (ECG) done also"*. I did not refuse. I was very appreciative of his concern. The doctor gave the green signal. I was perfectly alright, and I think Arjun felt quite at ease when he took me to the airport.

In the event, I had a very comfortable journey. I had made up my mind not to hesitate to seek assistance from the staff or co-passengers. I was highly impressed by Singapore airport, and realized how large and modern it was compared to Palam. I got to the lounge from where the plane to Brisbane would depart, but did not venture out to see the rest of the airport lest I got lost. But food and drinks were available and there were shops if one wanted to buy anything. I spent the hours window shopping as I really did not need anything.

I just bought a box of chocolates for Marcus. I was a little anxious that the plane should reach Brisbane in time as the gap between my reaching Brisbane and the departure of the plane to Honiara was just an hour. If I missed the connection, I would have to spend three days in Brisbane because the flight to Honiara was only twice a week. Much to my relief we arrived in Brisbane very much in time. I was received by the staff who conducted me to the transit lounge and later to the aircraft which was to take us to Honiara. We were a couple of hours late because we had to wait for a delayed connecting flight from New Zealand. I then realized that I had been apprehensive for no reason as had my flight been late, they would have waited for me also.

On reaching Honiara, I was received by George and Indu at the aircraft steps with a bunch of exotic orchids, the like of which I had not seen before (they are now available at a price in India). After Singapore airport, Henderson airport looked so small, much smaller than even Patna or Lucknow, which have only one runway. However, it did serve to connect Solomons to the rest of the world, which otherwise would only be accessible by sea.

We drove along a road which ran by the sea for three of four kilometres and then there was a steep climb. On either side there were well-built houses and the last one on the top was the European Community residence. The house was very spacious and beautiful. It was well lit. From the drawing room there was a view of the Pacific Ocean, and from the other window one saw mountains. It was a very unusual sight. I had always thought that the seaside meant plains because altitude is measured from sea-level, and the hilly regions were always far from the sea. It was a new vista for me. I had been to Kashmir, Darjeeling and Kasauli, which were far away from the sea, and Bombay and Goa which are situated on plains and are adjacent to the sea. On remarking about this unusual sight, the volcanic island of Savo was pointed out to me, which was visible from their verandah.

Honiara itself was quite small, but there were several other islands which were also part of Solomon Islands. My first impression of the place was that it was quite undeveloped. Coconuts and oil palms grew in abundance. I had occasion to visit the local market and found that they had many locally grown fruits and vegetables, even if the quality of the bananas was quite poor. However, there were a number of shops run by Chinese which catered to the needs of foreigners. There was one principal hotel at about three star level, but it was certainly enough for people to have a good meal or hold a cocktail party.

Considering that Solomon Islands was at such an early stage of development, I was surprised that it had diplomatic ties with the United States of America, the UK, European Union, Australia, New Zealand, Taiwan, and Japan. I naturally concluded that either the islands had great potential for trade or were of military significance. I knew that during the Second World War a very important battle was fought between the Americans and the Japanese. I also knew that all the diplomats were not there just to uplift the standard of living of the local people. However, I had not gone to the Solomons as a research scholar nor to write a travelogue. I was there to be with my children for a holiday and was happy to be with them and not get into any great study.

My stay was doubly enjoyable because Marcus was growing up. He was nearly five years old and attending a nursery school. He kept me quite busy and wanted to play with me. He would want to run a race with me and I really found it quite difficult to catch him. It was a delight to watch the glee on his face when he got to the den first. Story-telling at night became a routine, particularly if George and Indu were going out for the evening.

As there were several islands, George sometimes had to go on tour for a couple of days. On one such occasion, George suggested that Indu and I should visit the neighbouring country of Vanuatu, which was considered a fine tourist destination, while he was away in Fiji. So off we went to Port Vila, a two hour plane ride away. We stayed in a picturesque hotel which had several small palm-roofed cottages as accommodation, consisting of one or two bedrooms and a sitting room. The dining room and lounges were centrally located and used in common. Sea bathing was popular as there was a lovely sandy beach. I was much impressed and am glad to see from a recent visit to Goa that Indian tourism is also developing to a high level.

Before I left Honiara, Europe (or Schuman) Day was celebrated on 9 May. George and Indu gave a huge reception at the Mendana Hotel where the Governor-General, Government Ministers and the Diplomatic Corps were invited. I was naturally very happy to see George and Indu welcoming all the guests. I still remember how well George's speech was received. Once the formalities were completed, the event turned into a delightful cocktail party. Indu had taken the trouble of finding all the Indians who were in Honiara, and they were among the guests.

INDIAN SPRING

One Indian couple was Mr and Mrs Gandhi. He was the manager of the ANZ Bank and we later went to his house for dinner. Mr Gandhi's family had been in Fiji for several generations, but they kept up their ties with India. He had married a Gujarati lady who ran her home in a typical Indian style. When we were in her house, she took us to her Puja room which was beautifully decorated with *Diyas*[79] and pictures of Gods and Goddesses. She was a vegetarian.

Another couple was Mr and Mrs Rao from South India. He was posted there as a representative of Asian Paints. There were other couples of Indian origin who had lived in the Pacific much longer, and had ties with Fiji.

Indu threw several parties at the European Community residence. There was a fair amount of women's activities also. The ladies would get together and bring a dish, which was a specialty of their own country, and then exchange recipes. I joined the ladies' bridge group, and the Mahjong group as well. Another activity was handicrafts. A lady from New Zealand was the principal organizer, and we all did a little sewing, embroidery or patchwork. All I can say is that in this modest and remote town, these ladies had carved out a very interesting life for themselves.

After a most enjoyable six months, George and Indu were now starting off on their annual home leave. After a halt of three days in Bangkok, they put me on a flight straight to Delhi, while they flew on to England. The three days in Bangkok were very enjoyable, if a little hectic. We stayed in the Shangri-La hotel near the river. We did a lot of sight-seeing, including all the Buddhist pagodas. The atmosphere of Bangkok reminded me very much of Rangoon. The Burmese and Thai cultures are very much alike, particularly the temples with their colourful paintings, statues, and Buddhas in different postures. I was especially impressed by the reclining Buddha, and by the Royal Palace.

Life in Pune

By the time I returned from the Solomons, Pavan had already shifted to Pune. So after spending a few days with Praveen in Noida, and then at the farm with Brother, I flew to Pune.

Pune was now going to be our permanent home. Both Pavan and Shyama had decided to settle down here in their own flat in Salunke Vihar, so that the education of the girls would not be disturbed. Shyama also wanted to establish herself and get down to solid work professionally. Pavan had taken two years' study leave. When I reached I found the family nicely settled in their three bedroom flat.

The only drawback was that the flat was on the fourth floor, which was the top-most flat. This meant climbing the stairs was quite an exercise as no lifts had been provided. Being on the top floor had an advantage also, as the roof which was over two flats made it quite convenient for me to have my morning walk of forty-five minutes there.

Radhika was now in first year college. Malavika was at St Mary's Convent. Shyama had found a job in a placement company which she found interesting. Pavan had joined a two-year computer course on study leave from the Army. I was quite happy doing a little housekeeping and baking, and a little knitting. Very soon I found that there was a club about three minutes' walk from our flat, which was open to the residents of the colony. It was essentially a Rummy club and most of the members were retired Army officers and their wives. I immediately joined this Club and made some new acquaintances and friends. There were several other activities like Kitty parties, Kirtans and Satsangs which I could have joined where the meetings were held by taking turns in their homes. Shyama after a while had given up her job and started the work of placements independently from the house. I did not want to disturb her routine so I just restricted my activity to the Club. If I felt like entertaining my friends I took food from the house and had a nice party there. This gradually became a recognized way of entertaining by others members, and we now have parties in the Club which are most enjoyable and give a feeling of camaraderie, because the Club is so small that all the members are guests and there is no special selection of guests. Over the years, all the members have become very close to me and I can say that to all intents and purposes they are now my extended family. I have enough confidence in each one of them, that if I call upon them for any help, they will always be there by my side. Life was smooth. Shyama was enjoying her work and Pavan after two years was posted to Kashmir. Before he left, both my eyes were operated successfully for cataracts.

In 1993, Indu came to India. She was keen to have a small property either in Delhi or in Pune. Nobody encouraged her to buy a place in Delhi, which was getting more crowded and polluted day by day while prices were rising by leaps and bounds. The second choice was Pune where Pavan was going to be a permanent fixture, and I would naturally be staying with them. Pune was expanding in a big way. Lots of new buildings were coming up. Shyama had already identified a flat for her mother in Raheja Gardens. It was coming up with a landscaped garden and swimming pool, as well as a Club House. It was hardly a kilometre away from Salunke Vihar. So when Indu and George came to India, they flew here from Delhi and spent a couple of days and decided to book a flat in Raheja Gardens also. They got possession in 1996.

When they were here for a few days in 1995, with the help of Shyama and Pavan they chose the designs of the furniture they wanted. Shyama spent a lot of time attending to the details including the kitchen, electrical fittings and curtains. So that when George and Indu came in 1996 they walked into a well furnished flat. They had taken the trouble of selecting some fine pictures and crockery from England which gave the flat a very distinctive look. This is the flat where I now live.

After Pavan's study leave was over, he was posted to Kashmir which was a non-family station so we all continued to stay in Pune. Once when Pavan was here on his annual leave, he met with a car accident. Fortunately for us, one of his friends Colonel De Souza, who lived in the same building in Salunke Vihar, was passing by. When he saw a large crowd and a green Maruti he recognized it and made his way through the crowd to see what had happened. It is quite common for a crowd to gather but rarely does anybody come forward to help. Colonel De Souza found that Pavan was unconscious; he called an auto rickshaw, put Pavan in the vehicle and rushed him to the Military Hospital and straight to the intensive care ward. He then came home and told Shyama who rushed to the hospital. Fortunately Pavan had had a very narrow escape from serious injury. He was put through several tests, but there were just a few scratches and bruises, and he was home within a couple of days. The car was badly damaged and took well over three weeks to be repaired. God has his own way of saving. Colonel De Souza's help was very timely and in taking Pavan direct to the Military Hospital saved us a lot of hassle.

Between 1992 and 1996 I made a trip to Delhi and Darjeeling and another one to Mount Abu. Unfortunately I could not get to Darjeeling when my sister-in-law Savitribibi died. Sometime after that Shaktiji suffered a paralytic stroke so I was determined to go and see him. He was with his son Narinder in a tea garden where he was convalescing. This garden was about fifty miles away from Darjeeling. I knew that the tea industry provided lovely homes for their general managers and was very happy to see a well-maintained large house with teakwood furniture and exquisite curtains. What really impressed me was the way Narinder and Kumkum had made it near perfect with their own collection of silver, cut glass and driftwood pieces which Narinder had collected and chiselled into beautiful artifacts. He was a keen gardener and often won prizes for the best maintained gardens. Kumkum was most hospitable and I was very happy to see all the care that was being given to Brother.

The only thing lacking was good company. It was a lonely life, so both of them had developed hobbies, which kept them busy, and they never hesitated to drive 30 or 40 kilometres to attend a dinner with the manager of an adjacent estate, or go to Darjeeling for a day or for shopping in Jalpaiguri or Siliguri.

I went again to see him after a couple of years, this time with Nirmala. He was in Darjeeling in his own house Vernon Lodge living with his son (Vijay) and daughter-in-law (Sudha), who welcomed us and extended warm hospitality. It was after a gap of about twenty years that I had gone to Darjeeling. The house was looking more or less the same, but the town seemed to have lost its charm. It was very crowded, with shops on either side of narrow roads which made even walking difficult. In the olden days cars had to be parked once the tourists had reached Darjeeling and they were not allowed to ply on the roads. Only the Governor's car was permitted. Now the cars were moving all over the place adding noise and confusion. The standard of cleanliness had gone down and the only area which still had a little charm was the Birch Hillside. The Himalayan Mountaineering School was an attractive new addition. Thus I had the opportunity of meeting Surrinder, Narinder, and Vijay, the three nephews and their spouses. Asha, my brother Shaktiji's daughter, is the only one I have not met often, though I attended her wedding in Delhi and she is married to Arun Khanna, son of a friend of N.P., Nitya Nand Khanna, who came from Peshawar.

In February 2000, Shaktiji passed away, a couple of days after his grandson Aditya (son of Narinder and Kumkum) got married in Delhi. I was in Delhi and attended the wedding. Only Vijay, who had returned to Darjeeling after the wedding, was by his bedside. Narinder took a plane to be in time for the funeral. It reminded me of my father who also waited for his granddaughter's wedding to take place before he breathed his last.

I made a trip to Mount Abu to be with Nirmala in the Sanyas Ashram [80]. I enjoyed the simple regulated life and the illuminating lectures of Shri Maharajji. The morning and evening walks were most enjoyable, particularly around the lake which had several shops selling Rajasthani artefacts. This area was always full of tourists. The main attraction is the Dilwara temple, a Jain temple about 10 or 12 kilometres from Mount Abu. It was built much before the Taj Mahal and one has to see it to believe that such exquisite architecture in marble was built at such a high altitude so long ago. Anyone who has been to Rajasthan and not visited this temple has missed something in life.

Trip to Barbados

After finishing his study leave, Pavan was posted to Srinagar (Kashmir) for a couple of years. He then returned to Pune so the family was once again together. Radhika had finished her BA in commerce and a course in computers, and was trying to go to America on an exchange programme. Shyama was now well established in her work of placements and was taking keen interest in the NGO *Asha* which she had set up with her friends Maggie and Mira.

In 1995, George was posted to Barbados as Ambassador and Head of the European Commission Delegation for the Eastern Caribbean. On their way to their new posting from Solomon Islands, Indu and George spent a few days with us in Pune. Since Pavan and the family were now well settled, I readily accepted their invitation to visit Barbados in 1996. The plan was to go to England for a few days, attend the wedding of George's niece Elizabeth (Richard's daughter) and then proceed to Barbados. I was very happy to attend the wedding because it gave me an opportunity of witnessing a church wedding in England. It was a solemn ceremony, and the church had been decorated very tastefully with flowers. It turned out that the floral decorations had been done by the bride's aunts. This not only exhibited taste and talent, but also patience and perseverance. After the church ceremony there was a short recess followed by a lunch reception on a grand scale hosted by the bride's parents. It was a pleasure to hear George's speech when he proposed the toast to the newly-weds. The drive from Hove to Gloucestershire gave me an opportunity to see the English countryside in all its summer glory. The Downs reminded me of Ooty's grasslands.

On reaching Barbados, I was pleasantly surprised to find Bridgetown a modern developed city, quite different from Honiara. I knew that in former times, the West Indies had been under British rule, with labour imported from Africa and India for the production of sugar cane. I was not far wrong, because when we drove from the airport to Highgate House I found it looking similar to those places in India's tea gardens. In fact Highgate House, which was the residence for the European Commission Ambassador, had earlier belonged to a sugar planter. However, several new houses have been built on the surrounding land which was formerly the sugar plantation. Highgate House, built in 1740, had been visited by George Washington and later by Sir Anthony Eden. It is a magnificent two storied house, with spacious drawing and dining rooms and a large kitchen downstairs, with four bedrooms upstairs. Next to the kitchen was a guest suite, part of which Indu had turned into the TV and family room, while the bedroom was used mainly for storage of all the sports bats and balls. During my stay, George's sons, Julius and Nicholas also came to spend their vacation, and it was pleasing to see their interaction with Marcus and the family. I had met Christopher in Hove and I know that he is also very fond of Marcus. It is good to see over the years how the relationships have grown. Marcus is in his last year at The King's School, Canterbury, where he represents the school at cricket, rugby and soccer. His elder brothers are now all married and well settled.

Many of the people of Barbados are of African origin. A few are of Indian descent. Because of its reliance on tourism, there are many 5 star hotels, and the beaches are full of foreigners.

George and Indu had a busy social life with the diplomatic circle. Indu, as a member of Soroptimist International, did quite a lot of social work with them. It also gave her an opportunity to meet many of the prominent women in Barbados society. It was most enjoyable being in the house, which had its own swimming pool. Marcus was growing up and had joined the scouts. He had many friends who would come to the house for swimming. The garden was spacious with many Bougainvilleas which gave colour. Indu bought some attractive palms which were set around the swimming pool, besides adding lots of flowering plants to the garden. Among the trees in the orchard I was able to identify a mango tree and a Ber (Indian berry) tree, which did not yield any fruit, but I was able to gauge that some effort had been made to grow the Indian fruits, even if they were not there in abundance.

There was a lovely Indian temple which Indu and I visited several times in accordance with my habit of visiting a temple on the first Tuesday of every month. The local ladies were in charge of the temple and on special festivals like Navratras and Diwali they would have special Bhajan Kirtans. Generally the temple was open for about an hour every evening when one of the ladies would be on duty. On the whole I had a most enjoyable stay of nearly six months.

The only sad thing that occurred during this period was the passing away of George's Mother, who has been looked after for many years by her daughter

Brenda. We had a lovely Christmas Eve party and just as all the guests left we received a telephone call from Richard giving us the sad news. George's sons were with us, and we all naturally felt very sad. The funeral was to take place after a few days, and George flew back to England to be able to attend. I am told that both the brothers George and Richard read extracts from the Bible in voices that showed great regard for their mother.

I reached Delhi in February 1997 in time to be able to attend Gaurav's wedding (Kay and G.P.'s son) and then returned to Pune. Gaurav married Shivali whom he had known from school days. It was a wonderful event, tastefully organised, which I enjoyed thoroughly. I have always been very close to Kay and G.P. and their family.

Tragedy Strikes

On my return I found that Shyama was ready for a holiday and was more or less waiting for my return. She left for England some time in March to spend a little time with her Mother and sister. Neela, her sister living in America, was also visiting London. In April, Radhika was given an opportunity of going to America and she left via London to see her mother, before proceeding to the States.

Shyama returned to Pune in May. While in England she had consulted some doctors for her back ache which had been bothering her for years. The doctors did not find anything which might have required surgery.

It was Friday 13 June. The day passed off peacefully. The following day we read in the newspapers that there had been a fire in the Uphar Cinema in Delhi and about 60 people had been burned or choked to death. Most of those who had died were seated in the upper circle and were not able to get out quickly enough. In the evening when I returned from the Club, Shyama told me that there had been a telephone call from Delhi to inform us that Kartar Malhotra (Kusum's husband) had died in the accident. Even in my wildest imagination I would never have thought that Kartar could have been a victim. He hardly ever went to cinemas and to go to an afternoon show in the heat of June would seem impossible. It appears they were invited by a friend next door who had spare tickets for a very good film which was opening that day. There were five of them: the friend with his son and daughter, Kusum and Kartar. When the fire broke out the son just caught hold of Kusum and pushed her out. When he tried to re-enter to help the others, the heat and smoke was unbearable. Thus Kusum and this young man were saved, but the other three suffocated to death. It was a terrible thing to happen. I could well imagine the agony and anxiety that both of them must have gone through. Ashwan was in Hong Kong and Rashmi in Bombay. There were informed in time for them to reach Delhi for their father's funeral. The rest of the family was in Delhi and the Agra group also reached. I was not able to go, but found myself thinking and worrying about Kusum.

In my wildest dreams I did not imagine that yet another tragedy of a greater magnitude was to hit us.

It was 25 June. I returned from the Club at about 6.30 pm and found that nobody was at home. The servant told me that Sahib (Pavan) had gone out and on his return had received a telephone call that *Memsahib* (the lady of the house, Shyama) was ill in one of the shops downstairs, so both Pavan and Malavika had gone to fetch her. I could not make any sense of what he was saying, when Malavika came very excitedly and said *"Bari Ma, come Mummy has had a heart attack and is in hospital"*. I rushed down with her, the auto-rickshaw was waiting and we reached the hospital. She was in the Emergency ward where 3 or 4 people were attending to her. I only got a glimpse as they did not allow me to go in. Another doctor took Malavika and me to an adjacent room, while Pavan stayed with Shyama. Malavika then told me, *"Mummy had gone to the beauty parlour on Salunke Vihar road (hardly ten minutes walk from the house). When she had finished she decided to walk back. After a short distance she felt unwell, and walked into a shop. She sat down and requested the shopkeeper to ring up the house. She rang up and was told by the servant that Sahib was not at home."* Malavika had gone for her music lesson, Pavan had just gone to fetch her and on his way back had called at the beauty parlour but was told that Shyama had left. On reaching the house they were surprised to see that Shyama was not there, because they had not seen her on the road. Where had she gone? The telephone rang again, and was told that his wife was awaiting him in the shop. Pavan and Malavika rushed to the shop which was very close to the house, put Shyama in the car, and rushed her to the Military Hospital. Once Shyama was under treatment, Pavan sent Malavika home to fetch me. We reached the hospital but within ten minutes of our arrival Shyama had gone.

All three of us were stunned. We were like three statues as we sat in the car. Nobody knew what to say to each other. The news spread like wildfire. Within minutes the house was full of neighbours who were all very shocked. Some had seen her going down, one or two had even spoken to her for nearly five minutes, it had started drizzling, and she had taken an auto-rickshaw. Within minutes of our reaching home, there was a telephone call from the hospital asking if we would like to donate her eyes. Pavan responded in the affirmative. They then said that his signature would be required. Pavan said, *"In that case, do not delay, send the necessary papers, and I will sign"*. Thus the last good deed done by her was to give vision to someone who was blind.

Then started a series of telephone calls. Shyama's Mother and her sister Alka were in London. Radhika and Neela, Shyama's elder sister, were in America.

Indu was in Barbados. Besides these international calls, relations in Calcutta, Bombay, Delhi and Darjeeling were all informed. Nirmala had come down from Mount Abu to attend the thirteenth day ceremony for Kartar and was in Delhi. The whole night telephones were ringing to and fro. Dilip Kher, Shyama's cousin, and his wife Surekha, came over the same night and were a pillar of strength for the next three days. Nirmala, Praveen and Savita arrived next evening. Shyama's Mother and sister from England could not reach before 27 June so the funeral was fixed for that day. Neela and Radhika arrived on 28 June. Shyama's cousins came from Nagpur, Bangalore, Bombay, and Indore. Indu rang up several times but I stopped her from coming as George had undergone an emergency appendicitis operation a few weeks earlier and was still convalescing.

Pavan was determined to finish all the religious ceremonies by the fourth day. So although the funeral took place on the third day, on the fourth morning the ashes were immersed in a sacred river and in the evening the religious ceremony and prayers for the peace of the departed soul was attended by all the relatives and several friends. Neela, Alka and Savita left the next day as the two sisters had come without giving much notice, and Savita had left her little son

Aryaman with his grandmother. Praveen and Nirmala also went back after a few days and now only Radhika and Shyama's Mother were with us in the house.

It seemed as if Pavan had taken the shock bravely, for he was not weeping or moaning, but I knew how hurt and upset he was. To begin with he took a month's leave and within a week he put in his resignation. He said he did not want any more postings away from Pune. He decided to take over the work that Shyama had started. As a mother I could gauge how hard was the blow that had been dealt to him which had shattered his home life within minutes. I was hoping and praying that God, who had put us in this terrible situation, in His Grace would also give us the strength to bear this irreparable loss.

Radhika was here on a month's leave. Her boss was very sympathetic and told her that she was welcome to return, but if she decided to stay on in India, he would understand and not insist on the contract that she had signed. She wanted to return to America and Pavan did not want to interfere in her career. I also allowed her to decide for herself. So she went. I sometimes now think that had she decided to stay back in India her life would perhaps have taken a very different turn and even our lives would have been affected differently. If she had stayed on she could have been a much better companion for Pavan than Malavika, who was too young, whereas I was too old. But destiny is very strong. In America she was alone. After all, she also needed understanding, care and sympathy. Instead of getting all this from the family, she received it from Mateen who had been a close friend for several years. After a while he became indispensable to her and she chose to marry him.

I don't think anybody realized my loss. With Shyama's death, the anchor of my life was irreparably damaged. I was now 78 years old. After N.P.'s death, I had closed my home and shifted to Pavan. I made several trips to Delhi, Darjeeling, Mount Abu, and spent a lot of time with Indu wherever they were posted, but I always came back home to Pavan and Shyama who really gave me a sense of security. Now the tables had suddenly turned. Pavan was not his normal self. Radhika had left. Malavika who was extremely understanding and a lovely child was too young and needed care herself. My commonsense told me that I was not getting any younger, and I was certainly becoming physically and mentally weaker day by day. Just as I tried to put up a brave front after N.P.'s death, so I did even now. The day belonged to the family and my routine; the night was my own and I would fall off to sleep after being awake for hours, thinking whether we could have averted the tragedy in any way. But nobody can fight destiny. What had to occur did occur, and we were all left with just thoughts of ifs and buts.

After a few months, Colonel Atul Mehra came to Pune and settled down in Salunke Vihar quite near our flat. He and Pavan had been course mates and both Atul and his wife Shashi proved to be very good friends. We enjoy a very cordial relationship. I find Shashi very reliable and affectionate.

Radhika's Marriage

Slowly and steadily the pain was lessening. Pavan was finding his work interesting and was doing well. He was kept quite busy with his work and success added to his enthusiasm. But he became a home bird and did not socialize very much. Malavika was doing well in school and had several friends. I encouraged her to invite them to the house and visit them. She showed interest in music and joined a music school for piano lessons. She made rapid progress and Pavan bought her a piano so that she could practice at home. There was a little music in the house and the general atmosphere was much better. Radhika came home for a short vacation and Pavan threw a lovely party to welcome her. In general I can say that life was very nearly back to normal. For the first time I was now thinking of Radhika's marriage and on one of my trips to Delhi I ordered a diamond set to give her a good present when she got married. Then came another shock!

In 1999 Radhika broke the news that she had become a Muslim. I was stunned and I think Pavan was also shocked. I concluded that she had taken this drastic step so as to be able to marry Mateen. I tried my best to persuade her to change her mind. *"But I like the Islamic religion"* she said. I said to her *"How much do you know of Hinduism to take this drastic step. I suggest that you take a year off from your work, travel with me, and I will take you to the best Hindu scholars who will teach you about the religion you are abandoning"*. But it was all of no use. She was determined to marry Mateen, although she did not admit this in the beginning, but in 2000 she came up with the proposition of marriage. We knew it was not possible to change her mind, so as a father Pavan consented, but was still not ready to participate in the wedding. In all this confusion and commotion I felt like getting away from Pune for a while, for I thought Pavan was under great stress and my presence added to his confusion. At night I felt a peculiar pain in my chest, as if the heart was cracking, but slowly the sensation passed and I fell off to sleep. When I had this pain, I found myself thinking of Arjun who took the trouble of getting an electrocardiogram (ECG) done for me before I went to the Solomons. So it occurred to me that I should get an ECG done before I went to Delhi. Brother was already very seriously ill and I certainly did not want to add any further burden to Arjun. In the morning Radhika came to my room and said *"Bari Ma, get ready and we can go and buy your air ticket."* My answer was *"Yes, we shall go, but before buying the ticket I want an ECG done"*. So we both left the house and Pavan went to the station to receive Surrinder and Deepa who were coming to Pune. We went to the nearest doctor who took the ECG and after studying it he seemed hesitant to speak. So I said *"Please be frank, I am after all 81 years old"*. He then said *"It is not good"*. Radhika now said *"Come Bari Ma, let us go home"* to which the doctor replied *"Take her to a hospital instead."* This must have frightened Radhika and she enquired *"Which hospital?"* to which I replied *"The Military Hospital"*. She immediately rang up Pavan from the doctor's office and told him that she was taking me to the Military Hospital. We arrived at the hospital at the same time as Pavan, and I was put in the Intensive Care Unit where several tests were conducted. I lay there for about four days and was then shifted to the family ward. Praveen came immediately but since I was improving I told Pavan that Indu should come later. Indu and I came back to Raheja Gardens as the stairs of Salunke Vihar were a great deterrent. I returned to Salunke Vihar however when Indu returned to Brussels.

Radhika left for Dubai once I came home. She got married to Mateen there and proceeded to America. So she was all by herself in Dubai when she got married, although her Alka *Masi*[81] went there for a day to meet her after the ceremony. She had married with our knowledge, consent, and blessing, though not with our approval. I am very glad and relieved that she is happily married. She came to India with Mateen in 2001, and we welcomed them graciously. I have come to terms with her conversion and marriage, but still find her odd in wearing the *Chador* and covering herself with a black robe. I suppose with time I will get used to that also, for she continues to be the loving and charming Radhika we have always known. It is gratifying to note that her in-laws are very caring and she has adjusted herself very well with their ways and customs. Radhika is now the mother of two little sons, Eesa and Umar. For both deliveries, her parents-in-law went to America and spent some time looking after her.

MATEEN AND RADHIKA, 2001

EESA AND UMAR, OREGON, 2005

Departures

After the death of his younger brother Devji in 1999, my eldest brother Somji was deeply affected. I returned from the hospital at the end of August 2000, and in September my brother Somji passed away. Within a span of fifteen months I lost three brothers. Brother was 91 years old and his last year was bad. I took his death quite bravely because I realized that death came to him as a relief. It was not possible for me to travel. Pavan volunteered to go but I was a little hesitant to send him, because I was still on a lot of medicines and felt quite weak. Of all my brothers and sisters I had a special regard for him, perhaps because he was the eldest, and was something of a father figure to me. We were always welcomed by Brother and Bhabi. I have over the years felt his loss very much. Whenever I went to the farm in Delhi I felt as if I had come to my paternal home and now I had lost that also! As Arjun is the eldest nephew and was born while I was still in school, I have great affection for him, and I am equally fond of

Abhay, my father's great grandson from the Puri side of the family. I had occasion to spend a little time with Abhay when he had come to see Brother in 2000 during his last illness. I found so much resemblance between the father and the son. I highly appreciated the care he gave to his *Dadu* [82]. Brother would have been very happy to see him married because he did know that an Indian girl Kajri was his girl friend. Abhay has now got married and has a daughter whom I have yet to see. I was glad to meet Kajri several times when she was still his girl friend. Arjun proved to be a very devoted son, and Brother could not have asked for any better.

All my brothers had now passed away and I knew that Delhi would never be the same for me. My sister Sarlabibi was there but she was now more or less bedridden and we were not able to have sisterly chats that we once used to enjoy. With advancing age she had lost some of her zest for life, although she was still a strong willed woman and would make little of her limited physical capacity. The only time she became animated was when her daughters sang her favourite songs. She breathed her last in July 2004.

Sarlabibi continued to live in her own house after her husband's death, as her daughter Sumen and her husband Colonel Somesh Kapur (who had retired) were living with her. She received full care and affection from them. Besides that, Kusum and Tara were also in Delhi and they visited her regularly. Rajen and Gieta also decided to shift to Delhi once Rajen retired. He has built a beautiful farm house near Delhi. Sarlabibi was never lonely. A very good thing that happened during her lifetime was that they were able to get back their Sundar Nagar house, which for years had been under litigation. She shifted to this house just a few months before she died. It was a source of great joy to her to get back her property and her daughters are now living there. This property was left to them by their father. It is very gratifying that all three of Sumen's children won scholarships for studies in America.

Now, besides me, there is only Nirmala of the Puris of my generation. Kamlabibi passed away on 25 March 2005. She was 91, and had been well looked after by Rupa with whom she was staying.

The Nehru Dynasty

I will now turn to the Nehru-Gandhi family, members of which have been in the front ranks of politics for the last eighty-five years. Pandit Motilal Nehru was a Kashmiri Pandit settled in Allahabad and had a roaring practice as a lawyer. He was an aristocrat, rich and famous. He had two daughters, Vijay Lakshmi and Krishna, and a son Jawaharlal, who was educated at Harrow in England, and returned to India as a barrister. He was a brilliant scholar who was deeply influenced by the Russian revolution, and the ideals of fraternity and equality were deeply rooted in him. On returning to India he married Kamla Kaul, a young good-looking girl from a well to do Kashmiri Pandit family. She was educated in the sense that she had been to school and had been brought up in a traditional Hindu style, shy and soft-spoken. When her parents found Jawaharlal as their prospective son-in-law, they must have thought how fortunate their daughter was to find such a glamorous man. He belonged to the same community, was rich, handsome, and came from the most respected family of Kashmiri Pandits.

The parents-in-law were very happy with her. Jawaharlal was a kind man, but he was a great thinker and may not have found much intellectual companionship with his wife. Kamla gave birth to a daughter in 1917, and named her Indira. By 1919, Nehru came under the influence of Mahatma Gandhi and very soon joined the Swadeshi movement in right earnest. Kamla as a good and dutiful wife tried her best to fall in line with her husband and started taking interest in politics. Unfortunately her health failed her, and she could not keep pace with her husband. Indira, as an only child, could not have had an easy childhood, with an ailing mother, and a father who was too busy with the affairs of the country, and was in and out of jail because of his fight for Independence.

I have always felt that a woman can put up with a lot of adversity if she is sure that she is the primary consideration in her husband's life. Unfortunately, Jawaharlal, in spite of being a very good, fair and considerate husband, was not able to spend much time with her. She was sent to Switzerland for treatment, as money never posed a problem, where she had to stay by herself for long periods. Jawaharlal was now very attached to her and tried to give her a lot of support but she was too ill and sadly died at a young age.

I met Indira once in Shanti Niketan, Tagore's famous school, which I was visiting with a team from the DAV College delegation. I was still a school girl, but was able to notice that she gave an impression of being a quiet girl with a rather sad expression. She later went to Oxford, and after her mother's death, married Feroze Gandhi, a Parsi, who was in no way related to the Mahatma, but the name Gandhi has always given a sense of glamour to the public.

Indira was a strong woman and devoted much of her life to her father. Later, when she became Prime Minister, she was opposed by Vijay Lakshmi Pandit, Nehru's sister, who was against the Emergency. Vijay Lakshmi was also a very capable woman and had been High Commissioner in Britain and our representative to the United Nations when Nehru was Prime Minister. Indira further proved her grit when she refused to bow down to the Congress High Command and the Congress O was formed. The victory against Pakistan in 1971 gave her further encouragement and when her election was set aside, she did not hesitate to declare a State of Emergency to be able to hold onto power. There is a Punjabi saying that a lion cub can be brought up as a little lamb until such time that it is fed on milk, but once he has tasted blood he becomes ferocious and will not rest until he has established himself as the King of the Jungle. Indira's father was strong and autocratic but he was an idealist. He only had the welfare of the people at heart and worked ceaselessly for the benefit of the people. Hence nobody had the ability or desire to criticize him or doubt his integrity. But Indira was now ambitious and became quite autocratic. Banks were nationalized, and the Privy Purses which had been promised to the Princes when they agreed to join India, were abolished.

Indira thought that by trying to implement a modest social welfare programme, she would continue as the sole representative of the people. She miscalculated. Her removal showed a big vacuum in the upper set of leaders and Indira was given another opportunity to follow in her father's footsteps. This time, she committed the blunder of sending the troops into the Golden Temple, the most important shrine for the Sikhs, and was assassinated. Rajiv was made Prime Minister; people still had faith in the Gandhi name, and he was returned to power in 1985.

Rajiv was young and had not been active in politics. He possessed confidence and was well educated. The public expected him to follow in his grandfather's footsteps, because the oldies were now out, and Rajiv did choose some young people who would be able to put the country on a progressive path. For sometime it seemed as if everywhere there was a ray of hope. But unfortunately, his one defence transaction with the Swedish firm Bofors through an Italian intermediary, caused an uproar. Allegations were made about kickbacks.

Rajiv tried to bring in social reforms also, as people were keen to have one unified social law for everybody. The Muslim laws of marriage and divorce were different to the Hindu laws. Even the Christian laws on women's rights after divorce varied. The High Court had given a ruling in favour of Shah Bano, a Muslim woman, when she demanded maintenance from her former husband who had divorced her for no reason. The Muslims objected and Rajiv felt shy of executing the verdict, because he felt it would alienate the Muslims who would not vote for him. By 1988, the Bharatiya Janata Party (BJP) and some other parties had gained ground.

Rajiv lost the elections in 1989. The Congress still had the largest numbers but it did not command an absolute majority, and Rajiv decided to remain in opposition. Then a series of coalitions of smaller regional parties came into prominence. The first Prime

Minister was V.P. Singh who lasted less than a year. He was keen to implement the recommendations of the Mandal Commission which recommended 27 per cent reservation in services and educational institutions for the scheduled classes. The people reacted very strongly against this. A person with 80 per cent in the exams was disqualified because he belonged to a higher caste whereas a person with 30 or 35 per cent was accepted. The students were up in arms, which lead to the fall of the Singh Government. The other recommendations were educating the scheduled classes and introducing land reforms so that they could improve economically. But no proper attention was paid to these recommendations.

Singh was followed by Chandhra Shekar but he also did not last as Rajiv Gandhi withdrew his support, and fresh elections were announced in 1991.

Ever since the coalitions started, people do not hesitate to change their parties to suit themselves. Sometimes the electricity and telephone bills incurred by Ministers are published in newspapers. It is shocking to see such exorbitant bills which the government is paying. Foreign tours and heavy hospital bills for treatments abroad amount to crores. The Lok Sabha is responsible for passing the budget and whenever there arises a bill for adding extra perks to the members and raise their emoluments, the bills are passed without much opposition. It is surprising to see how many working days are wasted, in disturbances and walkouts. Where are the ideals of Mahatma Gandhi, who thought that the Rashtrapati Bhavan [83] should be turned into a hospital and the Ministers should draw a small token salary, as they should really be the *"Servants of the People"*.

A new word has been added to my vocabulary *"Scam"*: the fodder scam, the sugar scam, the steel scam, the stock exchange scam. They are all about corruption, where a handful of people make crores and the innocents suffer.

Small regional parties bargain for ministerial portfolios and are ready to withdraw their support at the slightest provocation. The main party, instead of working for the benefit of the country, wastes a lot of time appeasing their partners so as to remain in power. It would really be much better if only one party has an absolute majority and gets on with solid work! But it appears that this is a Herculean task with so many parties trying to get votes. Perhaps it would be a bit easier if regional parties showed their preference before the elections, then people would be better informed and vote accordingly. But this is only my surmise and may prove impractical.

While on an election tour in Tamil Nadu, Rajiv was assassinated by the Liberation Tigers of Tamil Eelam (LTTE), an organization which was fighting for an independent Tamil State in Sri Lanka. Rajiv had sent an Army contingent to Sri Lanka as a peace keeping force, which ended up fighting the Tamil Tigers. His assassination led to a sympathy wave for the Congress once again.

Narasimha Rao became Prime Minister, and held office for the next five years, although there were allegations that some members of parliament had been bought. His tenure started a little shakily with the demolition of the Babri Masjid at Ayodhya in Uttar Pradesh. The Vishwa Hindu Parishad asserted that it was a sacred spot for the Hindus where Ram Chanderji of the Ramayana was born, and the Mughal emperor Babar demolished the temple and built a Muslim Masjid there. A legal case was in court for several years but no decision had been taken. Efforts are made from time to time to reach a settlement out of court but nothing had come out so far.

Several economic reforms took place under the guidance of his Finance Minister Man Mohan Singh, which marks the start of the liberalization process. The Congress was keen to have Sonia as an active member but she in her bereavement kept a very low profile

INDIAN SPRING

and did not want to join active politics. Maneka, the widow of Sanjay, was keen but Indira had disowned her completely and she entered politics as a partner of the BJP. She gained a certain amount of popularity for advocating the cause of prevention of cruelty to animals. Her son, Varun, has joined the BJP.

The general elections in 1996 led to the defeat of the Congress once again. The BJP Government fell after 13 days. The United Front Coalition under H. Deve Gawda lasted for just under a year, when the Congress withdrew its support. I.K. Gujral stayed in power for about 18 months. Fresh general elections were ordered in 1999. This time the BJP came in as the largest single party, but still could not get an absolute majority. So Atal Behari Vajpayee had to get the support of several regional parties like the Akalis of Punjab, Telugu Desam Party (TDP) of Andhra Pradesh, and Trinamul Congress of Bengal. It must have been an uphill task to keep the support of all the regional parties by giving them Cabinet rank and plum posts. However the economic reforms continued. Bangalore and Hyderabad became important Information Technology centres. The Kargil victory was another feather in their cap. India had already become a nuclear power. Thus the National Democratic Alliance, as it was called, was able to hold office for a full five years.

Then came the general elections of 2004. Sonia Gandhi came out to work for the Congress. She adopted the style of her mother-in-law in both dress and speech. Her speeches were a little shaky in the beginning but very soon she was speaking Hindi fluently and went into the rural areas with promises of uplifting the poor. She was now a confident speaker who spoke from her heart and she thus became an idol of the rural population. The slogan of *India Shining* did not do the BJP much good. There was undoubtedly some economic progress, but it was restricted to the middle classes and the cities. Sonia never projected herself as the shadow Prime Minister and the Congress came in as the largest single party, followed by the BJP. The Congress was able to form a Government with the assistance of the Communist Party of West Bengal and the Communist Party of Kerala. Congress now had to choose the Prime Minister. Members were all keen to have Sonia as their leader. Sonia was already the President of the Congress Party, but she refused to become the Prime Minister. As a woman of foreign origin, it may have been difficult for the people of India to accept her as Prime Minister. She declined the post because she did not want any controversy arising which would in anyway jeopardize the position of the Congress. She nominated Manmohan Singh as the Prime Minister. This was the first time in history that the Prime Minister was nominated by the President of the Party.

This was an excellent choice. Dr Manmohan Singh is a non-controversial figure, known for his ability and integrity. He has no desire to seek power and fame and only has the welfare of the country at heart. The Congress has the support of the CPI(M)[84] of Bengal, the CPI of Kerala, and several other parties. They have agreed to a minimum programme and the Government is trying hard to stick to the economic reforms. How successful they will be and to what extent poverty will be removed is yet to be seen. The ideological differences between the Congress and the Communists are well known. How long will Congress be able to placate its allies? We can only hope that they will be able to do some good to the country. Will the United Progressive Alliance actually be united and progressive?

Thus by giving up the post of Prime Ministership, Sonia has endeared herself even more to the people of her adopted country, but still continues to wield power and even the Prime Minister has to listen to and abide by her advice. Her son Rahul is a member of the Lok Sabha. Time will show what his achievements may be. All that can be said now is that the Nehru-Gandhi story is the history of Indian politics of the last 85 years.

If someone asked me what was the contribution of Britain to India during their rule of nearly one hundred and fifty years, I would say that their greatest contribution was that they made India one unified country where a federal system of government was possible. At the time of framing the Constitution, with about twenty states and fourteen recognized Indian languages, they made unification possible by introducing English as the common link language. Queen Victoria's proclamation in 1857, when India became a part of the British Empire, was the promise of granting India self-rule under the "direction, supervision, and control" of the British Crown. Reforms were introduced in 1909 and 1919, but the 1935 Act really laid the foundation of the federal form of government, for which credit can be given to Sir Maurice Gwyer for drafting it. It meant a strong centre with a fair amount of autonomy to the States. Sir Maurice Gwyer was the first Chief Justice of the Federal Court of India and became Chancellor of Delhi University. Later, when the Constitution of India was being drafted, his advice was very valuable.

Observations

The next question is what have we achieved in the last sixty years? I think that the maximum progress has been made by the urban women of India. The movement for the emancipation of women was started well over a hundred and fifty years ago by Raja Ram Mohan Roy, and received further impetus from Swami Daya Nand in the latter part of the 19th century. The cruel practice of *Suttee* (the burning of childless widows on the funeral pyre of their husbands) was declared illegal and so was the practice of female infanticide. Education for girls was advocated and child marriages were discouraged, but the reforms were very slow.

Reforms gained momentum after Independence, as I have observed during my own life. My Mother was illiterate. Of her three daughters, two married while still in their teens, only I went to university, and all three of us remained as housewives. Of her granddaughters, Praveen and Indu did their MAs, and

Indu worked with the United Nations in New York, and later with the British High Commission in India. Two of Mother's great granddaughters are PhD's from America married to foreigners working abroad. Yet another is a graduate from Oxford, a postgraduate from Cambridge, and now works as an executive in an investment bank in London. Of my granddaughters, Savita is a fashion designer married and working in Delhi, Radhika is a computer expert employed in America, combining career and marriage. Malavika is still too young but is also on the right path doing an MA in Economics.

Earlier there were very few openings for women but today they are joining the Administrative Service, the Armed Forces and the Police. They have made very successful doctors, lawyers and business executives. They are present in politics and both houses of Parliament. They are distinguishing themselves in every field. Kiran Bedi of the Indian Police introduced remarkable reforms into the Tihar Jail in Delhi. Lila Seth, mother of Vikram Seth the famous writer, retired as the Chief Justice of Himachal Pradesh. Even in the field of science and technology they are noticeable. As early as 1983, Aditi Panth and Sudipta Sengupta were members of the scientific team that went to Antarctica. Kalpana Chowla of NASA fame has done India proud.

Legal reforms have also helped. The Hindu Law now insists that girls cannot be married off before the age of eighteen. Polygamy has been declared illegal and divorce is permitted. Laws of inheritance have also undergone change. If a man dies intestate all his children have equal rights to his property. These laws are restricted to Hindus (and Christians) only. The Muslim laws of Sharia governing inheritance still prevail and the Government so far has not been able to bring about a uniform code for all, in spite of being secular!

Too big a disparity between urban prosperity and rural poverty is a sad reflection on Indian society. Progress in the villages, where 70 per cent of Indians live, is still lagging behind. Until such time as the standard of living of small farmers is raised and the infrastructure of the villages improves we will continue to be regarded as a third world country. The Government has been aware of this since Independence, but now there seems to be a greater focus on rural areas, with more emphasis on education, health care, as well as water and electricity. Non-Government Organisations are also coming forward in spreading literacy, organizing small scale cottage industries enabling villagers to become more self reliant and economically independent. The task is gigantic but not impossible, for the villagers themselves are ready to learn and work hard. With proper guidance and assistance there will surely be further progress in narrowing the gap.

Raheja Gardens

For the last two and a half years I have been living in Raheja Gardens by myself. I cannot say that I am lonely. To begin with Indu came from England to settle me comfortably and then both she and George have been visiting Pune and spend a month or two with me every year. Praveen also visits me once a year and spends as much time as she can. Nirmala, my younger sister, who is now well above eighty, has visited me twice for two or three days. She does not like to travel by herself and takes the opportunity when her children come this side on business. Pavan and Malavika are always here, and I only have to ring them for anything I require, and they are promptly there to attend to my needs. Sakpal, Pavan's most trusted aide, is extremely helpful to me in household support services, and takes me daily to the Club. From time to time, when Pavan is away, Malavika shifts to me and I am happy to have her around. She has grown up to be a lovely girl and is well up in her studies. At the moment she is doing her MA in economics from the prestigious Gokhale Institute of Pune. Besides this she is very fond of playing the piano and has a lovely singing voice. She is an excellent driver and always makes herself available for every Sunday when Sakpal has his holiday, as I like to go to the Club every day.

In addition, there is the extended family of Brigadier Inder Sodhi, Reena Varma, my nephew Surrinder Puri and Deepa, Sanjeev Shekhar, son of Sheila and Raju, who all have places within a one kilometer radius. Even if we do not meet every day, I have the satisfaction of feeling that they are all nearby, and I can depend on them if I need any assistance.

In short, I can say that I am one of the very fortunate old people to receive so much love and affection from family and friends.

Reflections

It is said that the biggest lesson that history teaches is that it teaches us nothing. Humanity continues to make the same mistakes, so history has a knack of repeating itself. From times immemorial there have been wars in the name of religion, and yet no religion advocates violence and killing. All men are born equal, they are the creation of one God yet there is racial discrimination, instead of love and respect for all fellow beings, there is suppression and domination of the strong over the weak. It is a great stigma on twentieth century civilization that in the first fifty years two World Wars of long duration were fought. Complete cities with innocent men, women and children were wiped out by the Atom Bomb. The persecution of the Jews by the Nazi regime and the terrible happenings when India was partitioned are yet other examples of great human failure. The Berlin Wall which led to the breaking up and division of families eventually was broken down. A similar situation was created when the UN drew a Line of Control in Kashmir in 1947. Nothing has been resolved in the last sixty years and now efforts are being made to bring about goodwill by arranging special buses to enable people to meet each other.

During the last fifty years, there may not have been world wars, yet the war in Vietnam caused a great loss of lives. Even India has gone to war with Pakistan twice. Fortunately these conflicts were of very short duration, but who knows how long the unstable situation will continue in Iraq.

A very disturbing trend has now set in. Terrorism has gained ground. We have become used to seeing the destruction caused by bombs thrown at innocent people in the Middle East, Kashmir, India and Pakistan. Highjackings have been witnessed. The attack on the World Trade Centre in New York in 2001 caused great loss of life. It was fortunate that the White House itself escaped. Britain has not been spared either. It is imperative that this trend is curtailed. Terrorism to my mind is worse than war. At least when a war is declared there are two groups fighting each other and some norms are observed. Terrorism is a coward's way of fighting. Groups may later claim responsibility, but how does it solve any problem? We all know how painful it is for kith and kin to accept such tragedies.

Natural calamities have to be borne with a lot of fortitude, for they are beyond human control. Man's capacity to control nature is still very limited, which suggest that there is a greater authority ruling the Universe. We have to bow down to the will of God and try our best to mitigate the misery of those who have suffered natural diasters. Racial or religious discrimination is much more difficult to accept.

Unfortunately during the last few months the world has had to face a number of natural calamities. In December 2004 the Asian countries of Indonesia, Sri Lanka, Thailand, Maldives and India were hit by a tsunami. Thousands of lives were lost, the survivors were rendered homeless and the work of relief and rehabilitation had to be taken up on a war footing. It was gratifying to notice the response of other peoples in the world. Help arrived in the form of money, men and materials. Then came hurricane Katrina in America which caused loss of life and property, requiring further relief efforts. Just as I am on the verge of finishing my book I read the terrible news of the earthquake of great intensity which hit Pakistan and Kashmir on 8 October 2005.

It is feared that thousands have perished and thousands injured. Kashmir is a hilly region where access to villages is extremely difficult. The roads are blocked while the weather is a further hindrance with winter setting in. Help is arriving from all over the world. The Indian Army is working ceaselessly doing rescue and rehabilitation work. India is sending aid to Pakistan in the form of tents, blankets and food. Those who are injured, bereaved, and rendered homless will take a long time to recover from the trauma thay have experienced. Every cloud can have a silver lining. Can we hope that this calamity can bring India and Pakistan to a better understanding and become good neighbours?

Great masters have spoken about universal brotherhood, good will, love and respect for all life, human, animal and plant. Truth, non-violence, serving and mitigating pain and suffering have been stressed in different parts of the world, in different eras of history and in different languages. No religion defends killing, thieving, deceit or laziness. They all give a clarion call for universal brotherhood, love and service. Different disciples can reach the same goal, just as different rivers start from different sources become one when they merge and flow into the ocean. They lose their own identity and become one. Mahatma Gandhi and Mother Teresa are shining examples.

Mahatma Gandhi, an Indian Hindu qualified as a barrister from England, started an agitation against racial discrimination in South Africa and then returned to India to take up the cause against British Imperialism. He brought to the forefront the old Indian philosophy of truth and non-violence, acquired the qualities of a yogi, with non-thieving, non-hoarding and celibacy[85]. He wielded great influence over millions of people who were ready to sacrifice and even lay down their lives to gain Independence. His love for humanity was exemplary. He lived amidst untouchables and respected them. After Independence, his words were that he only fought British Imperialism but loved the British people.

Mother Teresa was born in Albania, a Roman Catholic by faith, who came to Calcutta as a young woman. She continued working in India for well over fifty years till she passed away in 1997. She worked ceaselessly for the poor, the diseased, the old and the dying, without bothering about caste, colour, creed or religion. She had so much respect for life that she set up homes for abandoned babies and tried to find suitable homes for them. Her work gained so much momentum that all over India the Missionaries of Charity have established homes for the poor, homeless and dying. In fact I had occasion to visit one in Africa. If we observe carefully we find that she had the same qualities that are required in a yogi. She was truthful and non-violent. She received enormous donations for her work but she had minimal needs and had no interest to acquire anything for her personal self. She embraced celibacy quite early in life. Thus by Indian standards she was also a great yogi who was loved and respected by humanity, and rightly has been beatified as a Saint by Christianity.

It is not possible for us all to attain the same heights, but if we make a sincere effort, and try to cultivate some of these qualities, a lot can be achieved. If we can do away with domestic and sexual violence and child abuse, a lot of unhappiness can be mitigated. Simlarly, if we try and give up greed which is the root cause of corruption and hoarding we would make very rapid progress. All these qualities do not need a high standard of education or great personal sacrifice. They only need a little thinking and can become a way of life.

With the advance in science and technology, the world has shrunk. No country can afford to live in isolation. If humanity is to survive, we must learn to live like a family and share the joys and sorrows of each other. This point has been stressed by old Indian philosophers who used the words *Vasudhai Kutumbum* *"The world is one family"*.

If I have drawn a rather dismal picture of the 20th century, I also note with great encouragement the shining examples of Mahatma Gandhi and Mother Teresa who worked in different fields but with the same qualities of love and respect for human life. They serve as torch bearers and it is up to us to follow their examples.

Generally, memoirs or autobiographies are written by people who have achieved some distinction in public life. The lives of politicians and spiritual leaders are written by their disciples, who also describe their teachings and achievements. In a way I am not really qualified to write my memoirs but am taking the liberty of doing so in order to give a short account of the times and tribulations that I have been through. The family gets a glimpse of the social and political thought of the 20th century, and the immense influence that science and technology have had. If a foreigner lays hands on this book, he or she would also get a fair idea of the life of an educated middle class Indian woman, her thinking and values. We are not all destined to do big things in life. I can only say is that I have tried to lead a clean, honest and truthful life, tried to give my children the right values, and have succeeded in giving three good citizens to my country, or I can use a wider term and say, citizens to the world. I have nothing to show for myself, but finish with the words of the Gita, the purport of which is:

"I accept with love, the loving offerings of my devotees, a leaf, flower, fruit or water for I know that a true devotee in his wisdom only does his duty and does not hanker for reward." (Chapter 10, Verse 26).

So I hope and pray that He will accept my petty effort of leading a simple clean life as a token of my devotion to Him.

Endnotes

[1] A kind of jasmine.

[2] Lala is a prefix indicating a Hindu Khatri, as Pandit indicates a Brahmin, Sardar a Sikh, Khan a Muslim.

[3] Father's younger brother's wife.

[4] Arya Samaj, a Hindu reformist movement.

[5] Punjabi script used in the Granth Sahib, the Holy book of the Sikhs.

[6] I refer to my eldest brother Som Prakash as Brother in this book.

[7] The youngest brother.

[8] A religious ritual with Vedic verses recited around a sacred fire.

[9] Devotional songs.

[10] A girls' school.

[11] They could only get their mother's things, which basically meant the jewellery that a mother possessed.

[12] Landlord.

[13] Nanny.

[14] A clay oven around which Indian rotis are cooked.

[15] Fish.

[16] The Great Mogul Emperor known for religious tolerance.

[17] Large Indian platters, made of metal.

[18] A gathering of people (Jalsa) in a garden (Jalliwala Bagh) in Amritsar.

[19] Indian New Year.

[20] Spinning wheel.

[21] Show.

[22] Bedspreads and rugs.

[23] Baton.

[24] Mother, there is no need.

[25] Gondola.

[26] Palanquin.

[27] Stablehands.

[28] Palanquin carriers.

[29] To be in the presence of the Deity or holy person.

[30] A phallus symbolic of the divine generative power of the god Siva.

[31] Obeisance.

[32] Nine auspicious days celebrated by Hindus all over India in different ways.

[33] A gift.

[34] Thaka and Shagan are gift ceremonies.

[35] Bridegroom's party.

[36] Departure of the bride.

[37] Rice and dal cooked together.

[38] A special train from Poona to Bombay.

[39] Gardener.

[40] Washer man.

[41] Motia is a kind of jasmine, Java Kusum a hibiscus, Gandh Raj, a gardenia, and Rajnigandha, a tube rose.

[42] Queen of the Night.

[43] Griddle.

[44] Exchange of garlands.

[45] Departure of the bride.

[46] One of the six schools of Indian philosophy.

[47] Verse.

[48] Molasses.

[49] An Indian herb.

[50] Le Corbusier was born Charles-Edouard Jeanneret in Switzerland in 1887. He adopted the name Le Corbusier when he moved to Paris in 1916.

[51] Flame Tree.

[52] A gathering of people for devotional songs and readings.

[53] Kohl.

[54] A sort of religious gathering.

[55] A religious ritual where Vedic verses are recited around a sacred fire.

[56] Durbar Sahib is the sacred book of the Sikhs and reading of it is called "path".

[57] Initiation.

[58] Victory to Mother.

[59] To be in the presence of a deity or holy person.

[60] The blessed food.

[61] Nankas means Mother's parents while Mammas means Mother's brothers.

[62] Silver or copper plates.

[63] A local dish.

[64] Hindu chant.

[65] Flowers.

[66] Eliminate Poverty.

[67] A Sikh group.

[68] A priest.

[69] Service.

[70] Exchanging garlands.

[71] Vegetables fried in gram flour.

[72] Behanji is a way of addressing an elder sister-in-law, Jijaji is brother-in-law.

[73] Chander, Inder and Sheila are the children of Prakash Vati and Prakash Chand Varma. Inder's wife is Reena.

[74] Earlier referred to as Swami Maheshananda Giri

[75] Devotional songs sung by a group.

[76] A gathering of song and dance.

[77] Maternal uncle and his wife.

[78] Red bangles.

[79] Oil lights.

[80] A Hindu monastery for monks, where lay people may also stay.

[81] Aunt.

[82] Grandfather.

[83] The President's residence.

[84] Communist Party of India (Marxist)

[85] Yoga Darshan, Satya, Ahinsa, Astaya, Aparigraha, Bhramacharya